A General Theory of the Price Level,
Output, Income Distribution, and Economic Growth

A GENERAL THEORY OF THE PRICE LEVEL, OUTPUT, INCOME DISTRIBUTION, AND ECONOMIC GROWTH

SIDNEY WEINTRAUB
Professor of Economics, University of Pennsylvania

GREENWOOD PRESS, PUBLISHERS
WESTPORT, CONNECTICUT

The Library of Congress has catalogued this publication as follows:

Library of Congress Cataloging in Publication Data

Weintraub, Sidney, 1914-
    A general theory of the price level, output,
income distribution, and economic growth.

    1. Prices. 2. Income. I. Title.
[HB221.W426 1973]   338.5'201   72-2574
ISBN 0-8371-6422-2

Trade Edition published simultaneously under the title "Forecasting the Price Level, Income Distribution, and Economic Growth"

Originally published in 1959 by Chilton Company
Book Division, Philadelphia

Reprinted with the permission of Sidney Weintraub

Reprinted by Greenwood Press, Inc.

First Greenwood reprinting 1973
Second Greenwood reprinting 1977

Library of Congress catalog card number 72-2574

ISBN 0-8371-6422-2

Printed in the United States of America

TO NEIL

Who Would Have Preferred a Book on Baseball

Preface

I have in these pages developed a glimmer of an idea that had been stirring in my mind for some time. As I worked with it, aided by the excellent statistics of the Department of Commerce, I found that the conceptualization was even more general than I had hoped. I think a single idea is able to unify important parts of the theory of the price level, output, income distribution and growth theory. Too, I think I have taken a necessary step to bring a compatible form of price level theory back into macroeconomics, an aspect which the late Lord Keynes in his giant contribution tended to neglect.

I must thank Professors Irwin Friend and Lawrence Klein for some suggestions that proved useful in securing quantitative data and numerous helpful remarks. Professor Klein, with his fine, quick intuition also encouraged me to a degree he could not suspect when one or two others almost dissuaded me from following through on my idea. Professors Richard Easterlin and Irving Kravis helped put the argument in better perspective. My students, Eugene Smolensky and Jan Dutta, performed several of the computations.

I am thankful to my wife Sheila and my older son Roy

for bearing with me during the trying period over which the manuscript was composed. I am indebted to the Staff of the Chilton Book Division for all possible publication aid.

SIDNEY WEINTRAUB

Philadelphia, Pa.
March 1959

Contents

A General Theory of the Price Level,
Output, Income Distribution, and Economic Growth

Introductory Note

In this study I think I have accomplished some important results for economic science. If I am right, the argument has rendered obsolete some major sections of economic analysis and has simultaneously shown the way toward a union and synthesis of several broad fields of our subject.

As I see it, my work has yielded the following results:

1. The law of the price level.
2. The unification of the theory of the price level and aggregate output and employment.
3. Some empirical laws of income distribution.
4. The influences on the price level in a growing economy and the synthesis of price level theory and growth theory.

I also like to believe that I have accomplished some further synthesis of analytic economics and empirical work, all toward the end of establishing an empirical science on a firm basis. If my arguments turn out to be acceptable, certain important institutions devoted to the task of economic stabilization will be affected. Too, I think my results contribute toward making economics a predictive science; my concepts can be used in forecasting. The margin of error and tolerance in certain important applications may not be any more than that prevailing in the physical sciences.

I have called the theory that I intend to elaborate a *General Theory* of the price level because the alternative theory that stems from the Equation of Exchange is, at best, a special theory. The latter is the relevant one in a pure exchange economy but not in a production economy in which output is continually turned out and in which market prices so substantially reflect wage and salary costs. In a pure exchange economy buyers with money confront sellers with goods, and the price level responds to the pressure of the money total and the willingness to spend it on the available goods. In a continuous production economy goods will not be produced unless costs promise to be covered and so, prices come to reflect costs and move with them.

While the central concept leads to the theory of the price level germane to a production-economy, it is also general enough to embrace simultaneously several areas of macroeconomics.

1

A New Predictive Theory

Truisms such as $MV = PQ$, $C + I = Y$, and $GC = s$ have played a not inconsiderable part in the development of our science. Generally speaking, they have enabled the economist to visualize rather complicated phenomena as being comprised of just a few major elements; they have also provided their share of intellectual fun in inciting some frequently exacerbating debate, in inducing fruitful conjectures on whether they hold or conceal new truths and real laws, and in maintaining a serene detachment from chronic endeavors to wring from them significant causal relations.

I think I have found a more useful truism than the $MV = PQ$ equation—one which is more susceptible to empirical verification and predictive application than this has proved to be. It will be my purpose in the following pages to justify this observation.

Two Tentative Laws

I propose to develop a tautology which covers the same general realm as the Equation of Exchange (hereafter EOE), and with the same purpose of specifying the major variables affecting the level of prices. Like the EOE, this one is also directly informative and illuminating, but its superior virtue is that it permits us to establish and incorporate certain empirical generalizations which aspire to the eminence of economic laws in the accepted sense, of testable hypotheses subject to verification. As part of the bountiful harvest of this approach, there are at least two propositions which present strong credentials for at least tentative elevation to the small and select peerage of economic laws. When one considers the limited members of this sect, this seems to be an unusual achievement. Almost inevitably, because of the difference in its approach, these important relations have been overlooked by those who attack price level phenomena through the EOE.

The Unity of Price Level Theory and Macroeconomics

I think my truism is also more congenial to many economists coming to the subject of the price level from general value theory, for its concepts are the familiar ones used in the theory of the firm and industry.* Too, it is entirely compatible with the various Keynesian brands of macroeconomics. To bless the union of these two, good data are conveniently accessible to compute its several components, and even to make independent tests of their magnitude, in a way not possible with the EOE where the velocity of circulation has always remained sternly aloof from direct measurement. These are the important claims which the analysis seeks to justify.

After defining the basic truism, which I shall call the *Wage-Cost Mark-Up* identity, hereafter abbreviated as WCM, through a minimum of fanciful detective work good estimates of the order of magnitude of the respective WCM components can be obtained; through the use of indexes the

---

* For a sample use of the basic idea to be developed, see my *Price Theory* (New York, Pitman Publishing Co., 1949), pp. 86–87.

argument leads quickly to the elaboration of two tentative empirical laws. I shall also indicate briefly how these ideas can be organized as an instrument for the prediction of future price levels, a not unimportant objective of economic analysis.

The "Source of Inflation"

Not least significant, the whole argument goes some way to remedy the recent criticism—not unmerited, I think—that Keynesian economics "provides no way of determining the source of inflation."* While my approach permits the marriage of price level theory to Keynesian economics—and I hope that I have been a good matchmaker—others may in the future be able to offer advice for an even more harmonious relation or suggest other partners. By indirection, at least, the argument will illuminate what has become the great controversy of this decade—to wit, whether the inflation has been wage-induced, with the cost-push dominant, or whether it reflects a demand-pull, with the money supply and its velocity being the active agents.

A Word on Scientific Laws

In order to understand the range of phenomena with which they deal, physical scientists attempt to relate the full complex of operative forces into some mental unity and then seek rules of behavior for the various component elements. A first rule often is to establish a balance of equivalents, or

* See Richard T. Selden, "Cost-Push versus Demand-Pull Inflation, 1955–57," *Journal of Political Economy* (February 1957), p. 5n. It ought to be observed that the EOE affords no way of "determining" the source of inflation, for the determining characteristics must come from behavioral or structural relationships; the EOE can only indicate the movement in components, and not the causal factors.

equations, as mathematicians describe them. To cite a very simple illustration of Newton's law of velocity of a falling body:

$$v = gt \tag{1.1}$$

Velocity is thus described as a resultant of two factors, a gravitational force (g) and time (t).

This is a statement of equivalence between v and its determining factors. However, our understanding was greatly advanced through experiment when the g variable was proved to be a constant, as $g = 32.2$. Hence:

$$v = 32.2t \tag{1.2}$$

This is a much stronger statement, for *we now have the law of g*. The detection of constants is thus always an important objective of physical science.

It is defeatist to contend that this method is inapplicable in economics because people are "volitional and sentient beings" rather than rigid static elements. Yet, in economic life, many relationships *are* rather hard and fast: not everything happens simply by chance or caprice. This proposition is particularly true in price phenomena. To decide in advance that durable relationships cannot be found in economics is not any more scientific than the attitude that varying relationships cannot be found.

The final test of any predicated relationship must be in its performance in predicting future events. Hence we do well to reserve judgment on whether a predictive—and simple—theory of the price level can be elaborated. I think it can. The following pages of this brief study show how.

A Remark on the Equation of Exchange

The equation of exchange has long been one of the profound simplifications of economic analysis; it still retains a widespread prestige though its history has been somewhat disappointing from the standpoint of a predictive science. The reason is not hard to explain.

The EOE may be written as follows:

$$MV = PQ \tag{1.3a}$$

$$\frac{MV}{Q} = P \tag{1.3b}$$

In both equations M represents the money supply and V the velocity of circulation or average turnover of each piece of money in the annual income process; Q denotes the volume of real output, while P stands for the price level.

The purpose of the equation is a simple one: it establishes a link between monetary phenomena, production, and the price level. The hope has always been that it could serve a predictive use and thus guide economic policy. Its crude application was embodied in the "quantity theory of money," which argued that any increase in the money supply would elevate prices. This overlooked the possibility that there could be simultaneous neutralizing changes in V and Q.

Even ignoring the difficulty of specifying M, of deciding whether only currency and demand deposits should be included, or whether it should also contain time-deposits and other money substitutes, past efforts have never been able to establish the constancy of V: the level of output Q is obviously not a constant over time. As a result, following changes in the money supply the price level has not always behaved as might be directly concluded from the formula. The source of the trouble has usually been recognized as residing with V. Obviously, as we have no way of counting the many daily rounds each piece of currency makes while it is in circulation, the velocity concept is not a quantity amenable to direct measurement. Indirect tests of V suggest that it is frequently volatile over even fairly short periods of time.

A superior theory would discard a variable which is so elusive and unsteady for accurate price level forecasts.

Price Level and the Value of Money

The practical importance of the price level has been impressed on everyone in this postwar decade of inflation. The price level is just another way of describing the value of money or, strictly speaking, its reciprocal. Thus, if prices double all around, the value of money is cut in half; if prices triple, the value of money falls to one third its former level. Schematically, writing P for the price level and B for the value of money, then:

$$P = \frac{1}{B} \tag{1.4}$$

Hence, with P going up, then B must go down.

2

The Basic Truism

Like the EOE, which proceeds originally from the simple truism that purchase outlay (MV) equals sales proceeds (PQ), we define the Wage-Cost Mark-Up identity from the only slightly less obvious statement that sales proceeds $(Z \equiv PQ)$ are equal to some multiple (k) of the wage bill, that is, of the money wage (w) times the volume of employment (N). The symbol Q will denote physical output while A will signify the average product per worker, so that $A = Q/N$. Thus, the following definitional equations can be developed:

$$Z = kwN \qquad \text{(2.1a)}$$

$$PQ = kwN \qquad \text{(2.1b)}$$

$$P = kwN/Q = kw/A = kR \qquad \text{(2.1c)}$$

This identity applies at the micro-level to each individual firm, with k constituting the ratio of mark-up of prices as against labor costs; its reciprocal is the commonplace computation of the ratio of labor costs to sales proceeds.* Because of its central importance in the theory that follows, we

* Formulas which reduce quickly to equation (2.1c) appear also in my *Approach to the Theory of Income Distribution* (Philadelphia, Chilton Company, 1958), pp. 51 and 69.

9

shall make frequent allusion to w/A, so that it deserves a term and name of its own: we will call it the Ratio (R).

The Analogy to the Law of Motion

Equation (2.1c), making allowance for the difference in meaning of its terms, is formally indistinguishable from the formula for velocity. In one, $v = gt$, in the other, $P = kR$. Is it possible to derive a value for k, say, similar to the 32.2 for g?

Within limits, we shall argue that this is the case.

The Availability of Data

Luckily, excellent data are available in the consolidated business accounts of the Department of Commerce national income estimates to give numerical significance to our concepts. Published estimates visualize the whole economy as one giant integrated business firm, thereby permitting the bodily transference of the WCM-concept, originally developed for the firm, into the aggregate economy. For instance, figures on Business Gross Product cover the sales of business firms in the aggregate, tantamount to the Z-term in the truism. Similarly, figures for the Compensation of Employees cover the same range of phenomena as wN, though a series free of salary elements would have been preferred. Directly from these figures it is possible to compute the value of k, or the average mark-up of sales proceeds over salary and wage charges. Likewise, a series on the number of full-time equivalent employees is published, representing our N. By dividing N into the employee compensation totals, the w-figures appear. All of the relevant series, before any processing, come from the statistical mines of national income information, carefully and imaginatively stocked and published by the Department of Commerce. All students of our economy are in their debt.*

The Task Ahead

The immediate job is to find data for the elements of the WCM-equation, specifically for the k, w, Q, N terms. Then we can appraise the order of magnitude of each element and the degree of stability in the path traversed by each in the past. Thereafter we shall want to consider the forces governing the change in each element. This last phase requires an understanding of the structural relations of the economy.

A Doctrinal Note

As a passing note, it is interesting to look at the famous truisms devised to catch the interplay of factors affecting the price level. The most renowned of them, the Equation of Exchange, stems in modern times primarily from Irving Fisher's celebrated volume in which the equation appears substantially in the $MV = PQ$ form, though separate currency and demand deposit terms are used by Fisher.† The most influential alternative expression is the Cambridge Cash-Balance equation, involving $M = \lambda PQ$, where λ signifies the portion of income that individuals want to hold in the form of cash.‡ Obviously, $\lambda = 1/V$, so that the two equations quickly merge into one, with the Cambridge equation

---

* I refer especially to *National Income* (1954 edition) and *U.S. Income and Output* (1959). The latter came to hand while this manuscript was being written.

† See Irving Fisher, *The Purchasing Power of Money* (New York, Macmillan, 1911). For the historical antecedents of the equation, see Arthur Marget, *The Theory of Prices* (New York, Prentice-Hall, Inc., 1938), Vol. 1.

‡ Alfred Marshall, *Official Papers* (London, Macmillan and Co., Ltd., 1926), pp. 52, 268. Also, J. M. Keynes, *A Tract on Monetary Reform* (London, Macmillan and Co., Ltd., 1923), Ch. 3.

placing more stress on the volitional elements affecting pur-
chase-expenditure decisions.

In his *Treatise on Money*, Keynes proposed a "fundamental
equation" based on wage earnings per unit of output and on
the discrepancy of Savings and Investment, with savings defined on the basis of an unsatisfactory concept of income
which excluded profits from the category.* Keynes aban-
doned this approach in his later volume.

These have been the main truisms which have sought
heretofore to come to grips with the theory of the price level.
As a new truism and a new theory are propounded, a passage
from Irving Fisher can serve as the keynote of the work:

"Truisms" should never be neglected. The greatest generalizations of physical science, such as that forces are proportional to
mass and acceleration, are truisms, but, when duly supplemented
by specific data, these truisms are the more fruitful sources of useful mechanical knowledge. To throw away contemptuously the
equation of exchange because it is so obviously true is to neglect
the chance to formulate for economic science some of the most
important and exact laws of which it is capable. [*The Purchasing
Power of Money*, p. 157.]

I accept Fisher's statement, deleting only the "equation of
exchange" and substituting the "wage-cost mark-up."

* J. M. Keynes, *A Treatise on Money* (New York, Harcourt, Brace and Co.,
1930), Vol. I, pp. 135–137.

3

The Partition and Measure of Elements

We now take recourse to the available data for calculating the components of the WCM-equation, thereby partitioning off the separate components of the price vector isolated in equation (2.1c). We begin with the figures for Business Gross Product, which we take as an obvious proxy representative of our Z or PQ category.

Business Gross Product

According to the Department of Commerce, its figures on Business Gross Product cover, in the main, "all private enterprises organized for profit."* This conforms almost perfectly to our Z-concept, especially when only an index of its movement will ultimately be required for our purposes.

Table 3.1 shows the totals for the Business Gross Product from 1929 through 1953. Statistics for employee compensation, by way of wages and salaries, are included alongside. This is as close as the data will take us to the wN-concept.

* *National Income* (1954 edition), p. 40. Also included are government enterprises and owner-occupied dwellings. Considering its coverage, and the fact that we shall want to make only index-number use of the concept, the category leaves little to be desired as an index of PQ.

TABLE 3.1.   BUSINESS GROSS PRODUCT, COMPENSATION OF EMPLOYEES,
AND MARK-UP FACTOR, 1929–1957*

Year	(1) Business Gross Product (billions of dollars)	(2) Compensation of Employees (billions of dollars)	(3) = (1) ÷ (2) Mark-Up Factor (k)
1929............	$ 94.8	$ 43.8	2.16
1930............	82.2	39.6	2.07
1931............	68.0	32.8	2.07
1932............	51.1	24.7	2.07
1933............	48.7	23.2	2.10
1934............	56.7	26.9	2.11
1935............	63.7	29.5	2.16
1936............	72.4	33.6	2.15
1937............	80.5	38.7	2.08
1938............	74.3	35.2	2.11
1939............	80.1	38.2	2.09
1940............	89.1	41.9	2.13
1941............	112.5	52.8	2.13
1942............	139.9	67.2	2.08
1943............	162.8	80.8	2.02
1944............	174.5	85.4	2.04
1945............	173.4	83.9	2.07
1946............	184.2	92.5	1.99
1947............	210.7	107.0	1.97
1948............	234.2	118.0	1.98
1949............	230.3	115.6	1.99
1950............	254.2	127.0	2.00
1951............	291.2	146.2	1.99
1952............	304.9	156.9	1.94
1953............	321.4	169.5	1.90
1954............	317.9	167.5	1.90
1955............	349.0	181.3	1.93
1956............	366.9	196.2	1.87
1957............	384.4	206.1	1.87

* Source: *National Income* (1954), pp. 168–169.
    U.S. Income and Output (1959), pp. 134–135, 138–139.

The depression of the 1930's and the great wartime and postwar prosperity expansion are reflected in these figures of Table 3.1. At this point we merely refer to the very high constancy of k, the mark-up factor. The entire next chapter is devoted to this subject.

Once more, definitionally:

$$k = \frac{\text{Business Gross Product}}{\text{Compensation of Employees}}$$

Average Compensation and Number of Employees

The basic WCM-truisms of Chapter 2 also contained symbols for w, N, Q, and $A = Q/N$.

This section presents data for w and N.

Available information on the average compensation per employee, and on the number of employees, is compiled from National Income rather than Gross *Business* Product data: hence the aggregate compensation figures differ (slightly) from the statistics of Table 3.1. However, as we seek only average compensation figures, the differences will be nominal, of a few dollars at best. Once we transpose the statistical facts to an index number basis, any remaining differences between them will inevitably vanish because of the rather full overlap of the two informational fields.

The close identification of column (1) in Table 3.2 and column (2) in Table 3.1 is apparent: the figures in Table 3.2 run a shade higher, indicating its more inclusive coverage.

The ravages of the Great Depression in terms of unemployment show up in Table 3.2. The growth in the working population and the economy since 1929 also appear. According to the statistics, average compensation (w), derived by dividing the total employee compensation by the number of

TABLE 3.2. COMPENSATION OF EMPLOYEES, NUMBER OF FULL-TIME
EQUIVALENT EMPLOYEES, AND AVERAGE COMPENSATION
PER EMPLOYEE, 1929–1957*

Year	(1) Compensation of Employees† (in billions of dollars)	(2) Number of Full-Time† Equivalent Employees (in millions of employees)	(3) = (1) ÷ (2) Average Compensation per Employee (in dollars)
1929............	$ 46.7	33.1	$1,411
1930............	42.3	30.9	1,370
1931............	35.1	27.7	1,266
1932............	26.6	24.3	1,097
1933............	24.8	24.2	1,026
1934............	28.7	26.6	1,080
1935............	31.4	27.7	1,134
1936............	35.6	29.7	1,199
1937............	41.0	31.6	1,298
1938............	37.4	29.3	1,276
1939............	40.5	30.7	1,319
1940............	44.3	32.6	1,360
1941............	55.4	36.3	1,527
1942............	70.1	38.9	1,805
1943............	84.0	40.0	2,099
1944............	89.1	38.9	2,290
1945............	88.0	37.3	2,357
1946............	97.0	39.4	2,464
1947............	112.1	41.4	2,708
1948............	123.6	42.3	2,922
1949............	121.4	40.7	2,983
1950............	133.4	42.0	3,172
1951............	153.0	44.4	3,449
1952............	164.0	44.9	3,649
1953............	177.0	46.0	3,845
1954............	175.2	44.5	3,938
1955............	189.9	46.0	4,130
1956............	205.5	47.3	4,345
1957............	216.0	47.5	4,548

* Source: *National Income* (1954), pp. 178–179, 196–197.
U.S. Income and Output (1959), pp. 200, 211.
† Includes all private industries plus government enterprises; excludes general government.

employees, fell from $1,411 in 1929 to $1,026 in 1933. In 1957 the average employee earned $4,548.

Table 3.2 thus yields information on w and N.

Real Business Product

Next, we seek to get a measure of Q.

When we reflect on the diversity of goods produced in our business economy, from toys to tractors and mules to Cadillacs, it becomes plain that they cannot be added in physical units. Only money, or dollar amounts of goods, can impart homogeneity to this mass of heterogeneous items.

To circumvent the difficulties economists and statisticians have created the concept of measuring each year's output of individual goods (and services) on the presumption that prices remain constant. This magnificent artifice yields the measure of the real output of the economy. Published statistics refer to such series as the Gross Product in Constant Dollars. Thanks again to the wonderful labors of the experts in the Department of Commerce, a series on Business Gross Product in constant dollars is available, extending back to 1929. This is a useful representative of our Q-variable in the WCM-equation. The series appears in Table 3.3.

The sharp descent in total output between 1929 and 1933 is reflected in the figures. The tremendous upsurge in the war and postwar periods is also apparent. The dip in the mild recession years 1949 and 1954 also obtrudes.

The Partitioned Price Level Matrix

Significant individual series have now been obtained for w, N, Q, and k. Thus the elements determining the price level have been isolated and partitioned. This has been done through the medium of statistical data pertaining to the

TABLE 3.3. BUSINESS GROSS PRODUCT IN
CONSTANT 1954 DOLLARS, 1929–1957*

(IN BILLIONS OF DOLLARS)

1929	$159.5
1930	143.2
1931	132.3
1932	110.3
1933	106.3
1934	116.3
1935	129.5
1936	147.2
1937	158.2
1938	148.4
1939	162.4
1940	177.9
1941	205.8
1942	225.1
1943	237.8
1944	251.2
1945	248.6
1946	244.1
1947	250.3
1948	260.4
1949	258.2
1950	281.8
1951	299.5
1952	308.7
1953	323.7
1954	317.9
1955	346.2
1956	354.1
1957	357.7

* Source: *U.S. Income and Output*
(1959), pp. 136–137.

world of phenomena in which we are interested. This is the economist's substitute for the laboratory and the experimental information derived by the natural scientist. The actual world is his testing ground.

Because the price level is couched in index number terms, we must compute simple index number series for each of our elements. This is accomplished simply by calling the value of the element in the base year (or years) 100, and then comparing the values in other years to the base year, and using the resultant figure as the relevant index. If an automobile cost \$1200 in 1939 and \$2400 in 1959, if 1959 is taken as 100 then the 1939 index is 50. Conversely, if 1939 were regarded as the base year, then the index series would be 100 and 200, respectively. A process as simple as this has been applied to our information.

For those unfamiliar with the price level concept a word further might be appended on its meaningfulness. Consider the infinite variety of goods and services produced in our economy. Since the 1930's and 1940's all of us are aware that prices have risen. How are we to measure this rise? It is no help to have *all* individual prices before you *; instead the price index serves as a clue to what has been happening to the purchase price of a fixed basket of goods over a period of time. It is the changing cost of such a basket of goods that is represented by a series of index numbers.

There are several things to notice about the index number series in Table 3.4, even at this stage.

First, there is the wide range of variability in w, the series denoting average wage and salary compensation. From a value of 49 in 1929 it struck a low of 36 in 1933; thereafter, it rose with some gradualness to the early prewar year 1941. Then it started an upward spurt in the tight labor markets

* This would swamp and overwhelm the analyst with too much detail.

TABLE 3.4. INDEX NUMBERS OF AVERAGE COMPENSATION, EMPLOYMENT,
REAL OUTPUT, AVERAGE OUTPUT PER EMPLOYEE, AND MARK-UP,
1929–1957*

(1947–49 AVERAGE EQUALS 100)

Year	w	N	Q	$A = Q/N$	k
1929	49	80	62	78	109
1930	48	74	56	76	105
1931	44	67	52	78	105
1932	38	58	43	74	105
1933	36	58	41	71	106
1934	38	64	45	70	107
1935	40	67	50	75	109
1936	42	72	57	79	109
1937	45	76	62	82	105
1938	44	71	58	82	107
1939	46	74	63	85	106
1940	47	79	69	87	108
1941	53	87	80	92	108
1942	63	94	88	94	105
1943	73	96	93	97	102
1944	80	94	98	104	103
1945	82	90	97	108	105
1946	86	95	95	100	101
1947	94	100	98	98	99
1948	102	102	102	100	100
1949	104	98	101	103	101
1950	111	101	110	109	101
1951	121	107	117	109	101
1952	128	108	120	111	98
1953	135	111	126	114	96
1954	137	107	124	116	96
1955	144	111	135	122	97
1956	151	114	138	121	94
1957	158	115	139	121	94

* Derivations of index numbers:
  1. w from Column 3, Table 3.2.†
  2. N from Column 2, Table 3.2.†
  3. Q from Table 3.3.†
  4. A from Q divided by N.
  5. k from Column 3, Table 3.1.
  † From original data, prior to rounding.

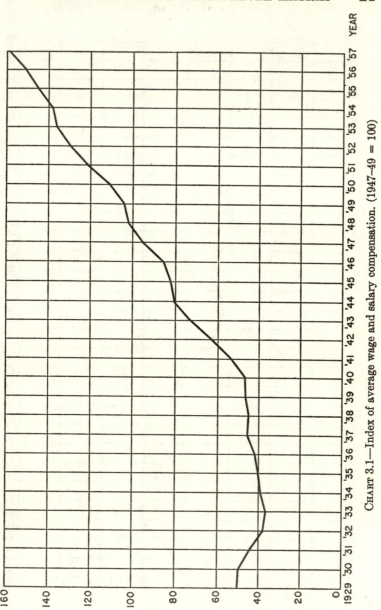

CHART 3.1—Index of average wage and salary compensation. (1947–49 = 100)

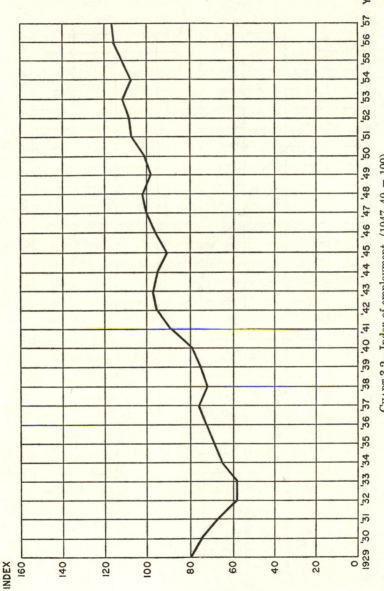

CHART 3.2—Index of employment. (1947–49 = 100)

that followed. Since 1944 the series has almost doubled, a pace of 6 index points per annum, on the average. The average wage and salary has, in the present vernacular for inflation, "galloped" ahead in the postwar years. The Korean episode in 1950–1951 shows a 10 index point rise. The movement of wages is shown in Chart 3.1.

Employment has fluctuated over a narrower range, being 80 in 1929, 58 in 1953, and 115 in 1957. Employment is thus a steadier element in our economy, as judged by the past, than the price of labor. The postwar movement is one of 15 per cent. This series is depicted in Chart 3.2.

The output series shows more variability than employment, but not as much as the average wage and salary compensation. Relevant benchmarks are: 62 in 1929, 41 in 1933, and 139 in 1957. A graph is drawn in Chart 3.3.

The figures on average product or average output per employee (A) are more stable still, in the sense that the dip or trough in the 1930's was not as deep as that in employment; at both ends of the scale, however, it was higher than the N-series. For 1929 the reading was 78, for 1934 it registered 70, and in 1955, the high year, it was 122.

The A-figures denote average product per head of the working force. The growth from 1929 to 1957 was 43 index points or 55 per cent.* Over the 28 years involved this means a productivity growth of 2 per cent per annum. This is to neglect the reduction of the work-week over this period. Average hours worked fell from 44 to 40, or about 9 per cent. Production would have been larger, per employee, if a general preference for more leisure had not been exercised.

Movements in the A-indexes are drawn in Chart 3.4. From 1946 the movement has been 21 points, or 21 per cent in this

* $43 \div 78$.

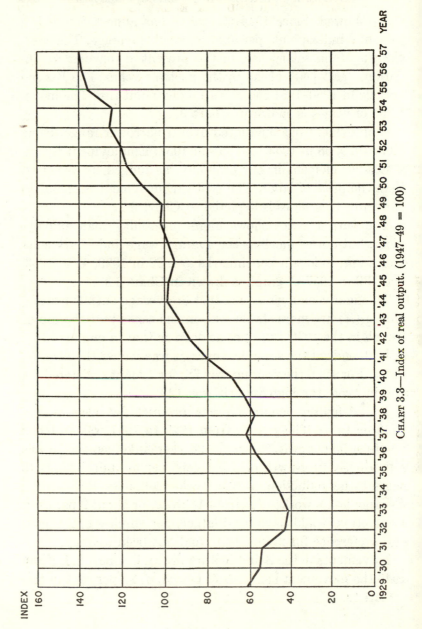

CHART 3.3—Index of real output. (1947–49 = 100)

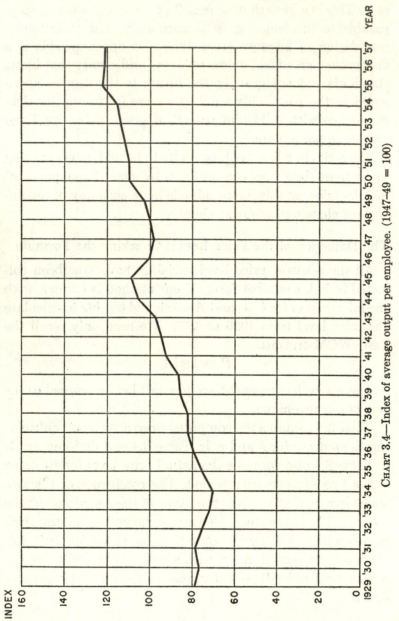

CHART 3.4—Index of average output per employee. (1947–49 = 100)

case. This is a growth of almost 2 per cent per annum, comparable to the longer growth since 1929. The cessation or retardation of advance since 1955 also appears. This is a dangerous sign which, unless reversed, will signify that living standards will not grow in the future to the degree experienced in the past. This could be a more fretful matter than experience with mild "inflation," of prices rising by 1 per cent or so per annum.

The series in k is something really to behold, never moving up by more than 9 per cent or down by more than 6 per cent. We shall discuss this minor miracle in an economy of revolutionary change in the next chapter.

The Detection of the Price Level: Checking the Formula

All the relevant price level variables have now been collected in index number form. If our method is correct, with the information for k, w, and A we should be able to calculate the price level from 1929 to 1957. We need only recall the basic WCM-truism:

$$P = kw/A$$

Values for each component are present. Let us proceed to the test of our technique.

Table 3.5 contains the computed price level from multiplying the indexes for k and w in Table 3.4 and dividing by A.

Table 3.5 also contains the actual price level for Business Gross Product over this period. The confluence of the two series is remarkable, a confirmation of the soundness of the method. The almost total identity of the two series, and their common merger along the time path, is shown in Chart 3.5. Even a large vertical scale, with a good vertical distance denoting an infinitesimal difference, will scarcely keep them apart.

TABLE 3.5. THE COMPUTED AND THE ACTUAL
PRICE LEVEL, 1929–1957*

(1947–49 AVERAGE = 100)

Year	Computed Price Level (kw/A)	Actual Price Level†
1929	68	68
1930	66	65
1931	59	59
1932	54	53
1933	54	52
1934	57	56
1935	58	56
1936	58	56
1937	58	58
1938	58	57
1939	57	56
1940	58	57
1941	63	62
1942	73	71
1943	77	78
1944	79	79
1945	80	79
1946	87	86
1947	95	96
1948	102	102
1949	102	102
1950	103	103
1951	112	111
1952	113	113
1953	113	113
1954	113	114
1955	114	115
1956	117	118
1957	123	122

* Source: *U.S. Income and Output* (1959), pp. 226–227.

† Implicit Price Deflators for Business Gross Product, converted from base 1954 = 100 to 1947–49 = 100.

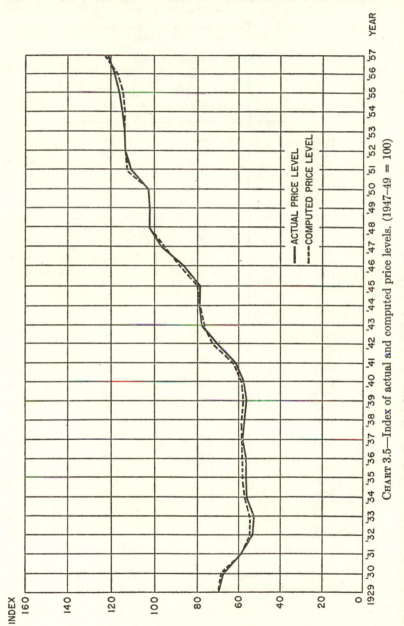

CHART 3.5—Index of actual and computed price levels. (1947–49 = 100)

Why the divergence of the two? There are three reasons: (1) While k and Q have been computed from the same universe of data as the actual price index, this was not true for w and N. Hence some difference is practically inevitable. (2) Differences would have been smaller, as a rule, if our calculations were carried out to more decimal places; we have dropped these, working only in round numbers. (3) Some similar, *and very trivial*, rounding off of estimates may be present in the Department of Commerce price series. Of these reasons, the first is probably the only significant reason.

Consider what has been accomplished. In effect, if the Department of Commerce published the data and failed to give us the price series involved, with a minimum of detective work we could ascertain this. In this sense, an important one, our method checks out.

Other methods can be concocted for this same purpose, of computing the implicit price series in the income data. The more important accomplishment is that: (1) *we have shown the elements influencing the price level and* (2) *we have shown the magnitude of importance and the range of variability of these elements.*

These have been the present achievements (up to this point) of our basic theory. It checks out. It can be useful, therefore, as a predictive tool. It can be useful, hence, as a guide to public policy in an age of inflation (or deflation).

The more solid accomplishments of the simple ideas painfully elaborated in this chapter will be developed in the two chapters to follow.

A Word on Predictive Tools

The Wage-Cost Mark-Up truism can serve as a predictive tool. It gathers together in simple conceptual form the important variables operating on the price level. It indicates the past order of size of these elements; with a minimum of imagination, a reasonable familiarity with the facts, and intelligent guess-work, its predictive usefulness and importance seem assured.

More will be said on this subject in Chapter 6.

A Remark on Scientific Method

A remark on scientific method will not be amiss at this place.

Recall the basic truism, $P = kw/A$. Can we say that a rise in w *must* raise prices? This would be valid only if k and A were constant. Conceivably, a rise in wages could (somehow, though it is not wholly clear how this would happen and certainly it is not inevitable that it should) lead to an offsetting rise in A. Prices would thus stay constant. Likewise, similar interdependence could hold between a rise in k and a fall in A.*

Similarly, a rise in A will lower the price level only if movements in k and w fail to offset this force. To predict how the price level will behave requires that we must specify the separate determinants of each component. We shall do this below, in Chapter 7 (and partly in Chapter 6).

It might be observed that statements that A rose by 2 per cent in the past and thus will rise in the same way in the future *may* be invalid: crude analysts often use data in this way, extrapolating past trends.† However, events in the past happened in an economic matrix in which k and w were inextricably bound up with A. Only if this fabric of events remains firm will the past growth rate persist.

---

* This would happen with diminishing returns under pure competition. See my *Approach to the Theory of Income Distribution*, pp. 102–103.
† Modern theories of growth often exhibit this same fallacy.

Likewise, assertions about the wage rate alone, and prices, are vulnerable to the same criticism. Events in the past reflect the interaction of the k, A, and w components.

The fallacy involved may be best exhibited by the equation of exchange and the crude quantity theory of money. Often arguing from the EOE it would be asserted that an increase in the quantity of money would raise prices (proportionately, added the more doctrinaire proponents). Yet this could be the case only if V and Q remained constant. They rarely did. Hence the quantity theory was—and is—a poor theory: it could not predict the price level consequences of changes in the money supply.

I think, for reasons to which I now turn, that the WCM-truism yields better predictions, requiring less information and more accessible information.

4

The Law of k

Several times we have alluded to the high constancy in k, the mark-up factor of employee compensation in the basic formula.

Hitherto we have been told to peek at it but not look at it too closely. Now we want to scrutinize it from every direction, with full undistracted attention and absorbed fascination. *It is probably the most important economic law, in the true sense, that economists have to work with.* It is an unmatched empirical fact of the state of affairs in our economy which literally defies explanation. And yet it holds.

Consider what its unparalleled constancy and rigidity signify. The United States economy in the 1930's went through the deepest depression of our industrial history. The period was marked by important legislative changes affecting our economic pattern. In the 1940's we experienced the greatest of modern wars. There were price controls, regulations, and onerous rates of taxation. Since the close of the war we have had high prosperity and mild recessions.

Through all this the k-factor has gone its course, hardly changing the path that somehow guides it and keeps it steady in rough economic seas. What is the explanation? Good ones are lacking.

TABLE 4.1. ABSOLUTE AND INDEX VALUES OF k,
THE MARK-UP FACTOR, 1929–1957
(1947–49 = 100)

Year	Absolute Value	Index Value
1929............	2.16	109
1930............	2.07	105
1931............	2.07	105
1932............	2.07	105
1933............	2.10	106
1934............	2.11	107
1935............	2.16	109
1936............	2.15	109
1937............	2.08	105
1938............	2.11	107
1939............	2.09	106
1940............	2.13	108
1941............	2.13	108
1942............	2.08	105
1943............	2.02	102
1944............	2.04	103
1945............	2.07	105
1946............	1.99	101
1947............	1.97	99
1948............	1.98	100
1949............	1.99	101
1950............	2.00	101
1951............	1.99	101
1952............	1.94	98
1953............	1.90	96
1954............	1.90	96
1955............	1.93	97
1956............	1.87	94
1957............	1.87	94

To those skeptical of economic laws in the same sense as in the physical science, this one ought to prove a revelation. Here in social phenomena, of volition, caprice, and individual and social dynamics, there does seem to be some inexplicable reason, almost an economic necessity to its law of motion.

A Gravitational Constant?

Is the parallel to Newton's gravitational constant g far-fetched? Judging by the past, the comparison is not wholly overdrawn. Of course, its constancy is less; there is flex, there is some resiliency. But it is *highly* constant, if not *wholly* constant. And, unless strange distortions occur in our economy in the future, it is likely to hold rather firm; nothing visible on the horizon promises to upset it, or to transform k from a literal constant to a jumpy, nervous variable.*

The discovery of this constant—and it has been known in other contexts previously—is a finding of first-order importance. So far as I am aware, it has not been previously applied to the theory of the price level.

To refresh our memories on the movement of k, its absolute and its index number values are drawn together in Table 4.1.

The Constancy of k

As shown, the absolute value of k has fluctuated between a high of 2.16 in 1929 to a recent low of 1.87 in 1957.† That

* For one thing, if it changed it would convey a completely topsy-turvy reshuffle in the distribution of income among broad social groups. Societies hardly change in this way.

† Recent revisions of national income data, in *U.S. Income and Output* (1959) tended to raise slightly all of the figures on Business Gross Product for the years 1946 through 1953. I would not be surprised if this happened again when fresh information became available to the Department of Commerce analysts. If so, this would put the k-figures for 1956 and 1957 closer to their historical norms. Even so, the down-move is slight, compared to other series.

is, from the lowly plateau to the high peak, the difference has been 0.29. And all this has encompassed an incredible 29-year epoch. This is a most astonishing fact.

Other evidence indicates that something very much like the same empirical law operates in the English economy, and in the United States economy even prior to 1929.*

When one looks at the index number values of k it is even harder to repress excitement over this finding. Over the 29-year period, the maximum rise compared to the 1947–1949 average was 9 per cent. The lowest fall was one of 6 per cent. For 29 years it has hovered about this small range of variation.

Charts 4.1 and 4.2 show diagrammatically the limited variability of this element. We can conclude that k is a steady bird, of straight habits, and only very small transgressions. Important past legislative changes and tax changes haven't moved it very much from its path.

A Curiosum

Curiously, k registered higher in the depression years than in the 1930's. In the present prosperity years it doesn't seem to approach its 1929 value. Why? This question would be worth answering; yet we have no answers to it.

Why should k tail off in an era of high profits and high taxes? The subject begs for detailed investigation; economists have been remiss in not delving into the issue, and extracting either fresh evidence or new hypotheses.

The Comparison to Other Data

The k-factor rose to 9 per cent above the base year as a ceiling, and fell 6 per cent for the floor.

* See below, this chapter.

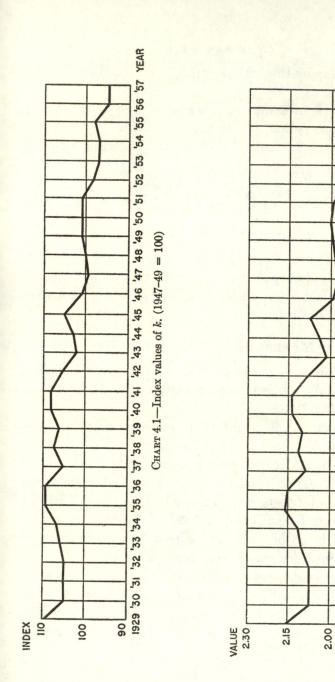

INDEX

CHART 4.1—Index values of k. (1947–49 = 100)

VALUE

CHART 4.2—Absolute values of k, 1929–1957.

Let us compare this with the other index number variables in Table 3.4.

The wage figures were at a low of 36 and a high of 158 over this same period, and on the same base.

Employment fluctuated between a low of 58 and a high of 115.

Real output (Q) ranged from 41 to 139.

Average product (Q/N) had a high-low cycle of 122 and 70.

Fifteen index points separate bottom and top k-values. The spread for the wage element is 122. For employment it was 57, for real output, 98, for average product, 52.

For economic series, we conclude, k is as *nearly* a constant as we are likely to find.

Year-to-Year Movements

Fascination with k and its constancy is even enhanced when we study the year-to-year movements. These are assembled in Table 4.2.

The frequency, and height, of the recorded changes can be neatly tabulated.

In 8 of the 28 year-to-year measurements there was no change in k. That is, on the evidence available, in 28 per cent of the cases there was no annual change in k. With the plus or minus 1-point cases, a total of 15 readings are included and in 53 per cent of the past 28 cases a guess of practical constancy would have been justified.

If a 2 per cent index change is regarded as on the small side—and I personally would be inclined to regard it so—in 21 of the 28 cases, or 75 per cent of the instances, a prediction of constancy in k would have been borne out by the unfolding facts.

TABLE 4.2. ANNUAL INDEX POINT
CHANGES IN k, 1929–1957

Year	Annual Change
1929–30	−4
1930–31	0
1931–32	0
1932–33	+1
1933–34	+1
1934–35	+2
1935–36	0
1936–37	−4
1937–38	+2
1938–39	−1
1939–40	+2
1940–41	0
1941–42	−3
1942–43	−3
1943–44	+1
1944–45	+2
1945–46	−4
1946–47	−2
1947–48	+1
1948–49	+1
1949–50	0
1950–51	0
1951–52	−3
1952–53	−2
1953–54	0
1954–55	+1
1955–56	−3
1956–57	0

Taken all in all, I think the evidence is clear: the practical constancy of k is an empirical fact.

This has a bearing on price level phenomena which ought always to be kept in mind in prediction and policy. Only rather fantastic changes in the economic structure are likely

TABLE 4.3. FREQUENCY DISTRIBUTION
OF YEAR-TO-YEAR INDEX NUMBER
CHANGES IN k

No. of Index Points	Frequency
−4	3
−3	4
−2	2
−1	1
0	8
+1	6
+2	4

to alter it—and if it altered there would be fantastic changes in our structure!

A Historical Note

When one reflects on it, economists ought to have been prepared for the results that have been derived on the remarkable past stability of k. For this finding is of the same order as the facts on the apparent rigidity of the wage share in national income, which was published by Kalecki about twenty years ago.[*]

Kalecki found that in Great Britain the relative share of manual workers in the national income seemed to stay put at from 40.7 per cent of the total to 43.0 of the total in the whole period from 1911 to 1935. For the United States his results were fairly similar, though they ranged lower. While

[*] Michal Kalecki, *Essays in the Theory of Economic Fluctuations* (New York, Farrar and Rinehart, Inc., 1939), pp. 16–17. A recent "doubting Thomas" on the constancy thesis is Robert M. Solow, writing "A Skeptical Note on the Constancy of Relative Shares," *American Economic Review* (September 1958). Nowhere in his measures, so far as I can see, does Solow use Gross Product or Gross Business Product. His criticisms thus belong to national income concepts. Further data for the United Kingdom appears in E. H. Phelps Brown and P. E. Hart, "The Share of Wages in the National Income," *Economic Journal* (June 1952), pp. 276–277.

he does not fully elaborate on how his calculations were derived, his evidence indicates a "manual labor" wage share of the national income between 1919 and 1934, hovering between 34.9 and 39.3 per cent of the total.

On an ingenious *a priori* analysis Kalecki argued that the constancy in income shares was due to a fortuitous growth in monopoly power which, somehow, just by happenstance counterbalanced productivity influences. The conclusion that there is a "self-adjusting" monopoly mechanism is scarcely a luminous and transparent fact considering that, tucked into our k-factor, are the proceeds necessary to cover income, excise, and property taxes, as well as depreciation, profits, and interest income required to enable business firms to continue in operation.

If one argued in this fashion, and associated k (which is not exactly equivalent to Kalecki's use of terms) to the degree of monopoly power, then we would have to conclude that, since 1945 and the general abandonment of the wartime controls, monopoly forces in our economy have diminished, with little wobbles in the tendency between 1946–1947 and 1954–1955. Also, that rather big changes in the measure have occurred since 1955.

All this is doubtful in the extreme. Evidence is hard put to support the theme that monopoly influences are either weakening or strengthening in our economy.*

The Postwar Sag in k

Even after the initial surprise, and blessed with the ex post wisdom which reminds us that the highly stable k was "not

---

* I would prefer to infer that the constancy of k constitutes a confirmation of an earlier argument I advanced to predict the constancy of the labor share *even under purely competitive conditions.* See my *Approach to the Theory of Income Distribution* (Philadelphia, Chilton Company, 1958), Chapter 3. My argument is tenable at least over the short period and would not be inconsistent with some drift in k over a longer period.

really unexpected after all," when one looks at its movement after 1945 the tendency of the mark-up factor to sag is a fact that, I think, could not have been predicted by *a priori* reasoning. For this heaviness in k has traversed a period in which "demand-pull" inflation has been widely described, an era in which consumer goods were in short supply, and a series of years in which a sellers' market has prevailed. When one compares this record with the depression 1930's, the downturn is even more astonishing: in the depression years the average mark-up through the economy seems to have been greater, despite the buyers' market and the pressure to expand sales. What with the enormous growth in the level of corporate income and excise tax levels the results seem rather quixotic, and invite detailed investigation.

Deserving of at least passing notice in this discussion, and bearing on the movement in k, is the fact that executive salaries are also components of the series on Compensation of Employees, and thus influence the computed w. Good evidence to correct the series is scanty and hard to come by; it is but a surmise that the increase in executive salaries outstripped that in ordinary wage income. Those with more familiarity with the data, and possessing more dexterity with its processing, might do much to enlighten us on this point.*

* Shortly after this was written, an estimate by labor union economists came to hand which bears on this matter. According to their evidence wages rose from an index of 100 in 1947 to one of 143 in 1953; for salaries the rise was to 137, and to 161 and 167 respectively by 1957. Thus the evidence is hardly clear-cut on the move in the average wage as against the average salary. However, the wage portion of the total seems to have fallen from some 76 per cent to 65 per cent by 1957, so that executives comprised a greater part of the labor income total. More work ought to be done on this; the basis, and acceptability, of the labor unions' wage-salary dichotomy is not very clear. See, however, Solomon Barkin, "Maximum Employment and a Selective Economic Control Policy," p. 42, in *The Relationship of Prices to Economic Stability and Growth: Commentaries* (Washington, American Federation of Labor, March 1959).

Conclusion

In 21 of the last 28 years, a forecast that k would not change by more than 2 index points would have been borne out by events.

This is perhaps as close as we are ever likely to come to finding a constant in the world of economic phenomena.

So long as it holds, might it not be useful as the "magic constant" of economic analysis?

5

The Law of the
Price Level

The near-constant k is one element in our WCM-truism. We can now consider R, the w/A ratio. This leads to another interesting relationship.

Briefly, it establishes the tentative law that the price level will rise only if R rises. This generalization approaches in significance the empirical finding on k. This one is a compound law which builds in an allowance for the synchronous movement in both elements rather than dependent on strong rigidity, as in k.

Correlation of w and A

Before linking R to the price level, Table 5.1 shows the annual index number changes in w, written Δw, and in A, written ΔA. The basic data are computed from Table 3.4. Thus, if A moves down from an index of 78 to 76, then ΔA is written as -2.

The data in Table 5.1 are interesting. Paying no attention to the absolute amount of the changes, in 21 of the 28 cases—that is, 75 per cent of them—both the average pay envelope

TABLE 5.1. YEAR-TO-YEAR INDEX NUMBER
CHANGES IN AVERAGE COMPENSATION
AND IN AVERAGE PRODUCTIVITY
PER EMPLOYEE, 1929–1957

Year	Δw	ΔA
1929–30	−1	−2
1930–31	−4	+2
1931–32	−6	−4
1932–33	−2	−3
1933–34	+2	−1
1934–35	+2	+5
1935–36	+2	+4
1936–37	+3	+3
1937–38	−1	0
1938–39	+2	+3
1939–40	+1	+2
1940–41	+6	+5
1941–42	+10	+2
1942–43	+10	+3
1943–44	+7	+7
1944–45	+2	+4
1945–46	+4	−8
1946–47	+8	−2
1947–48	+8	+2
1948–49	+2	+3
1949–50	+7	+6
1950–51	+10	+0*
1951–52	+7	+2
1952–53	+7	+3
1953–54	+2	+2
1954–55	+7	+8
1955–56	+7	−1
1956–57	+1	−0*

* Zeros preceded by plus or minus indicate
what additional decimal points would reveal.

TABLE 5.2. THE RATIO INDEX SERIES,
OF *w/A* INDEX NUMBERS, 1929–1957
(1947–49 = 100)

Year	R
1929	63
1930	63
1931	56
1932	51
1933	51
1934	54
1935	53
1936	53
1937	55
1938	54
1939	54
1940	54
1941	58
1942	70
1943	75
1944	77
1945	76
1946	86
1947	96
1948	102
1949	101
1950	102
1951	111
1952	115
1953	118
1954	118
1955	118
1956	125
1957	131

and average productivity moved in the same direction. In two cases, 1937–1938 and 1956–1957, the contrary move was very small, and might be neglected.

Let us assess the significance of this. As both Δw and ΔA tend to move together directionwise, the result is to hold the Ratio R more constant than if one moved without the other. If the Ratio is correlated strongly with price level up-swings, it will be because Δw exceeds ΔA when both are positive, and is closer to zero than the change in A when both are negative.

The Ratio Series

We shall want to utilize the R, or unit wage-cost, series of index values. These are incorporated in Table 5.2. They can be calculated from the earlier w and A values.

As would be expected, R neither dips nor advances as much as the w-series on compensation, but falls below the A-series till 1948. In the years since 1949 R has turned on steam, and has been above A. This is merely an affirmation of the fast pace of movements in the w-series. Chart 5.1 pictures the R- and A-series.

The Correlation of R and P

Let us now correlate the movements in the Ratio w/A (written ΔR) and in the price level. We look for the moment only at the signs, rather than the absolute changes. Also, because we have *two* price levels, the actual and the computed (with a shade difference between them) we will include both: ΔP will denote changes in the Commerce Department figures, and $\Delta P'$, changes in our computed price series (see Table 5.3).

The results of Table 5.3 are suggestive. Of the 28 readings there is correlation in direction 21 times. *From 1940 to the*

INDEX

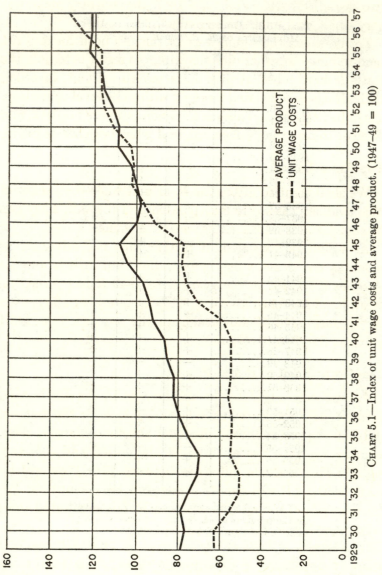

CHART 5.1—Index of unit wage costs and average product. (1947–49 = 100)

TABLE 5.3. DIRECTIONAL CHANGES IN INDEX
MOVEMENTS OF R, P, AND P', 1929–1957*

Year	ΔR	ΔP	$\Delta P'$
1929–30	+	−	−
1930–31	−	−	−
1931–32	−	−	−
1932–33	−	−	−
1933–34	+	+	+
1934–35	−	+	+
1935–36	−	+	−
1936–37	+	+	+
1937–38	−	−	+
1938–39	+	−	−
1939–40	−	+	+
1940–41	+	+	+
1941–42	+	+	+
1942–43	+	+	+
1943–44	+	+	+
1944–45	−	+	+
1945–46	+	+	+
1946–47	+	+	+
1947–48	+	+	+
1948–49	−	−	−
1949–50	+	+	+
1950–51	+	+	+
1951–52	+	+	+
1952–53	+	+	+
1953–54	+	+	+
1954–55	−	+	+
1955–56	+	+	+
1956–57	+	+	+

* Where 0 is registered in actual index changes
in the previous table, + or − indicates changes
reflected in significant decimal places.

*present, involving 17 annual readings, in 15 cases the move-
ment was the same, directionwise.* The lesson seems plain,
surely, for these last 17 years: a rise in prices always (90 per
cent of the time) accompanied a rise in the Ratio. This does
point to at least a *tentative* law of the price level.

Refining the Analysis

Let us look at the 7 cases since 1929 when there seemed to
be some contrariness or perversity to this law. Some of the
instances can be thrown out as quite meaningless in the sense
that the contradiction was so small as to be disregarded.

Examining Table 5.4, there appears new support for this
finding: the apparent contradictions of the "law of the

TABLE 5.4. ABSOLUTE CHANGES IN INDEX NUMBERS
FOR THE APPARENTLY CONTRARY CASES

Year	ΔR	ΔP	$\Delta P'$
1929–30.....	+0*	−3	−2
1934–35.....	−1	+0*	+1
1935–36.....	−0*	+0*	−0*
1938–39.....	+0*	−1	−1
1939–40.....	−0*	+1	+1
1944–45.....	−1	+0*	+1
1954–55.....	−0*	+1	+1

* + or − indicates changes reflected in significant
decimal places.

price level" are so tenuous and unimpressive that they can
be disregarded. Of the 7 cases, in 6 cases only 1 index point
difference is involved—a rather pseudo contradiction that
can easily occur because of minor perturbations in k.

If we tried to refine our index numbers and carry them to
several decimal points, this demonstration of the triviality
of the so-called exceptions would be more strongly confirmed.

The only real contradiction occurred between 1929 and 1930. But that was a year in which k fell from an index of 109 to 105, a rather sharp descent. The temporary instability of k distorted the effectiveness of the law of the price level—to wit, that changes in the R-factor carry the price level in the same direction.

The Degree of Correlation

The conclusion was reached that, of 28 readings, 21 complied with the "law of the price level." Six cases of apparent contradiction were eliminated because the magnitudes were trifling. Only 1 case thus ran contrary to the law. This was explained by an uncommon year-to-year degree of instability in k.

Let us look closer at the magnitude of the correlation between ΔR and ΔP.

Chart 5.2 depicts R and P. As the index levels so closely approximate one another, there is no need to convert year-to-year changes in percentage form: the use of raw index point changes will prove sufficiently accurate to make the relevant points.

Chart 5.2 is a "two-way" table, showing index fluctuations in R, P, and P', respectively. As we have two price levels, a circle will signify the association of ΔR with ΔP, the Commerce figures, and an x will indicate the ΔR and $\Delta P'$ correspondence.

The showing of Chart 5.2 is rather fantastic. Of 52 plotted points, 17 of them fall along a line of *perfect* fit. Of the computed price level points, where 28 are involved, 9 fit perfectly; that is, in almost one third of the cases a 1 point change in the index (1947–49 = 100 base) of R meant a 1

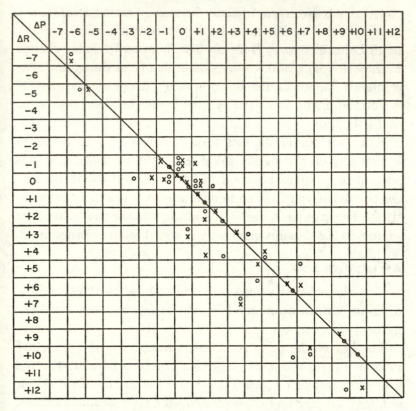

CHART 5.2—Changes in wage costs and the price level.

point change in the price index. For ΔR and ΔP the perfect association holds in 7 of the 28 cases.

Not only is the direction of changes in R and the price level assured, but also there is a strong, persistent likelihood that a 1 or more point change in R will be identified with an equivalent index number change in P.

Is this so surprising? Is it too perfect a relationship to be true? I think not. Consider how the P and R indexes are constructed. Both are initially in money terms so that a 1 index point movement in P, say, represents \$2 while a 1 point index change in R means \$1. Thus, a two dollar change in the one accompanies a one dollar change in the other. This is merely, again, a reflection of the "magic constant" k.*

For those who want the tabular facts, these are presented in Table 5.5.

When we look at the sum total of variations, the evidence is similarly on the significant side: positive variations in ΔR add up to 84 index points, to 74 for ΔP, and to 70 for $\Delta P'$. On the negative side, the figures are 16, 18, and 14, respectively. For argument's sake, therefore, it is not too far fetched to associate a 1 point change in P to a 1 point change in R.

A Tentative Law

Consider what has been achieved: we are on the threshold of an important economic law, equivalent to the laws of the natural sciences.

The law of the price level seems plainly to be that a rise in R will raise the level of prices. This must be interpreted intelligently: some *minimum sensible* for the R movement is entailed. It may be "contradicted" for microscopic changes; but these are never troublesome, in either prediction or policy.

One is tempted to go even farther and predict the order of variation in the price level for a given change in R. In the past, at least, this has been extremely close to 1 point to 1 point.

Thus we have extracted a new *empirical* truth or "law" in the proper operational sense; to wit, that a price rise can occur only if there is a rise in the Ratio, of average compensa-

* See Chapter 13 below.

TABLE 5.5. ANNUAL CHANGES IN R, P, P'
INDEX SERIES, 1929–1957*

Year	ΔR	ΔP	$\Delta P'$
1929–30.......	0	−3	−2
1930–31.......	−7	−6	−6
1931–32.......	−5	−6	−5
1932–33.......	0	−1	0
1933–34.......	+3	+4	+3
1934–35.......	−1	0	+1
1935–36.......	0	0	0
1936–37.......	+2	+2	0
1937–38.......	−1	−1	0
1938–39.......	0	−1	−1
1939–40.......	0	+1	+1
1940–41.......	+4	+5	+5
1941–42.......	+12	+9	+10
1942–43.......	+5	+7	+4
1943–44.......	+2	+1	+2
1944–45.......	−1	0	+1
1945–46.......	+10	+7	+7
1946–47.......	+10	+10	+8
1947–48.......	+6	+6	+7
1948–49.......	−1	0	0
1949–50.......	+1	+1	+1
1950–51.......	+9	+9	+9
1951–52.......	+4	+2	+1
1952–53.......	+3	0	0
1953–54.......	0	+1	0
1954–55.......	0	+2	+1
1955–56.......	+7	+3	+3
1956–57.......	+6	+4	+6

* Addendum:
 Total sum of $+\Delta R$ variations: 84; $-\Delta R = 16$.
 Total sum of $+\Delta P$ variations: 74; $-\Delta P = 18$.
 Total sum of $+\Delta P'$ variations: 70; $-\Delta P' = 14$.

tion to average productivity, or vice versa. This is a testable proposition capable of being falsified, and thus an appropriate hypothesis for economic science.* So far as I am aware, it has never been put in this form and applied to the theory of the price level. It has been totally bypassed by those who approach the price level problem from the armory of the Equation of Exchange.

The Logic of the Law

What is the logic of the law? Does it accord with common sense—which includes the corpus of economic reasoning?

In the simplest terms R, or w/A, boils down to a statement of the labor cost of production, per unit of output for each good. Is it not plausible to expect that, when this rises, that prices will rise?

I think so. Hence, what has been accomplished here is to take this homely truth from the theory of the firm—and common sense—and apply it to the economy.

It is fantastic that such reasoning has not developed hitherto with respect to the price level. What was lacking was the basic WCM-truism: this has provided the key and unlocked the price level door. When combined with the "magic k," all else falls in place. Economists have been looking too intently, and too mystified, at M's, V's, and Q's. They have missed the significance of the k and R.

---

* As Milton Friedman declares: "The only relevant test of the *validity* of a hypothesis is comparison of its predictions with experience." He goes on to say that the test may also be made in terms of events that have already occurred, so that "if a search of the records reveals that such and such did happen, the prediction is confirmed." I think the "Law of the Ratio" passes this test remarkably well. See his *Essays in Positive Economics* (University of Chicago Press, 1953), pp. 8–9.

6

On Predicting the
Price Level

With a correct theory prediction is a relatively simple
matter. If a physicist has his equations correct, the results
will check out. I think this is likely to be so for the price
level in the future. Now that we have a conceptualization of
(1) the basic truism, (2) the law of near constant k, and (3)
the strong tentative law of the price level, the remaining
tasks are not difficult.

When the data are not at hand for the immediate past in
the form which I was fortunate enough to have had because
of the labors of the Department of Commerce, economic
statisticians will know how to turn, twist, and shape other
curves and quantitative facts to serve as proxy representa-
tives for the better information they require. The following
brief remarks, however, may serve to acquaint those less informed as to the availability of good, current statistical
series and assist them in price level forecasting work.

The remarks are meant to be merely indicative of what
might be done. One or two more general observations on the
subject of prediction may also serve a purpose.

The Implicit Assumption of Extrapolation

A word on extrapolation in economic forecasting.

Prediction involves guess-work as to the size of economic variables in the future. With intelligent, informed analysts it is an intelligent surmise premised largely on the proposition that the future will be like the past.

This is the implicit assumption of the process of extrapolation. This refers to the practice of the forecaster of assuming that past trends, especially of the recent past, will persist. It consists of saying, for example, that if population has been growing at 2 per cent per annum it will continue this growth rate. Or if employment has been advancing at one half per cent per quarter, this will persist. Etc.

What is the philosophical basis for this? It is simply the belief that events do not fluctuate erratically, that the future holds some fastness to the past, especially the recent past. Ultimately it can be decomposed into a belief about the inner constancy of events, or the continuity of phenomena.* The same presupposition of uniformity lies at the basis of prediction in the physical sciences so that in this sense economics is not unique.

To deny this premise is to deny the possibility, I suppose, of any science. For short movements there are many variables that can be treated as constants in economics, or subject to moderate growth. The beauty of the "magic k" is that this has stuck to its path for an almost unbelievably long period.

---

* For some parallel remarks, compare my *Approach to the Theory of Income Distribution*, p. 56, where I refer to it as the "continuity postulate." I think that the too empirically minded, in their criticisms of economic theory, forget that they often are working on the same ultimate premise.

A Complete Price Level System

Let us now turn to the relationships that we need to complete our theory of the price level. The economist refers to this as the specification of the full system. Essentially, it amounts to indicating that there is, or can be, sufficient information to determine each element of the range of phenomena that is embraced by the argument.

We have so far been given the definitional WCM-identity. Subscripts in the equations indicate the time-dating involved. Thus t_0 denotes the present or future date for which we are predicting or striving to find a solution. The subscript t_1 would then indicate the following and t_{-1} would signify the preceding period of time.

$$P_{t_0} = k_{t_0} w_{t_0} / A_{t_0} \qquad (6.1)$$

Equation (6.1) contains four separate terms or four unknowns. To predict P_{t_0} we would need to find values for k_{t_0}, w_{t_0}, and A_{t_0}.

For k_{t_0}, the "magic constant," the equation is simple. This is equal to a (nearly) fixed value 2, or, in purer mathematical fashion, $\bar{k}$ or k_{t-1}. Thus:

$$k_{t_0} = k_{t-1} = k \qquad (6.2a)$$

Recognizing k as only *nearly* constant, we can insert a "drift-item" such as ϵ which is the best guess as to its near term movement.

$$k_{t_0} = \bar{k} \pm \epsilon \qquad (6.2b)$$

Equation (6.2b) is the better one. From fragmentary data on changes in mark-up ratios in important industries in the most recent past, some idea on the size of ϵ can be ascertained.

For A we can assume with fair accuracy—for very short periods such as a quarter year—that this is unchanged. Thus:

$$A_{t_0} = A_{t-1} \tag{6.3a}$$

For annual forecasts it would be better, to judge by past experience, to incorporate an upward lift in A. Letting r stand for the annual rate of rise, then:

$$A_{t_0} = (1 + r)A_{t-1} \tag{6.3b}$$

In practical work the growth term r can be estimated at about 2 per cent. This has been the experience since 1929. Various pieces of current information, such as indexes of output and employment, can be made to yield valuable clues as to whether the immediate past growth rate is slowing up, accelerating, or holding to a traditional pattern.

We now have three useful equations, (6.1), (6.2b), and (6.3b). We need one more equation to settle the system. This means an equation for w.

One obvious solution in a model in which unions seek to placate their members by an annual money wage advance would be to write, as in equation (6.3b):*

$$w_{t_0} = (1 + c)w_{t-1} \tag{6.4a}$$

This could guarantee "creeping" or "galloping" inflation, depending on whether the c-term is small or large. If it were 2 per cent, and A grew by 2 per cent, the price level could hold firm. If $c > r$, prices ought to mount, and vice versa.

Slightly more general would be to make the wage level contingent on past wage and price phenomena, to yield a

---

* In all the equational forms we seek, to accompany k and A, the average wage and salary compensation figure is intended. If salaries move differently from wages, separate terms must be included.

series in which wages always lagged behind prices; to explain past data this would not have been a bad simplification. Thus:

$$w_{t_0} = w(w_{t-1}, P_{t-1}) \tag{6.4b}$$

A more general form would be to insert a term for unemployment (U) and for the expected price level (P^*), to emphasize that union leaders and businessmen keep an eye peeled on the state of the labor market in striking the wage bargain. The relevant function would then read:

$$w_{t_0} = w(w_{t-1}, P_{t-1}, U_{t-1}, P^*) \tag{6.4c}$$

The interesting part of relation (6.4c) is that it can generate a wage-price spiral whenever $P^* > P_{t-1}$. Like the other forms of the equation, this also ties wages strongly to past events or historical events, rather than to present market phenomena. We shall comment on this shortly.* With any of these formulations, so long as they conform to the facts on evolving wage phenomena, a complete system with every element determined would result. There would be four equations to match up with the four unknown terms.†

From the Particular to the General

Clearly, w_{t_0} in the functional equations (6.4) refer to the economy, to the average wage, or to use with k and A, the average wage and salary compensation. Thus we have to inquire how the formulae may be used in connection with a wage settlement in particular industries,

* See Chapter 7, below.
† For equation fitting, the forecaster might profitably consult the excellent volume of Lawrence R. Klein, *A Textbook of Econometrics* (Evanston, Row, Peterson and Co., 1953).

As this is written, there is talk in the air of coming wage negotiations in the steel industry. The President has delivered the expected exhortations to both parties to exercise restraint, to avoid a wage rise that would lift steel prices and, thereby, other prices.

This is to see part of the problem. The usual addendum is that monetary policy can prevent the inflation. This is to misunderstand monetary policy and the significance of the conceptual patterns.

The problem is this. We must estimate the extent to which a rise in steel wages alters the *average* wage and salary compensation through the economy. Further, if steel prices rise, the average mark-up in other industries over and above wage and salary costs will rise.

Therefore, we have to estimate how much the change in the wage bill in steel will alter the total wage bill. Then, with the figures on employment in this industry, an estimate for the average w can be prepared.

If 2,000,000 men are involved* and the wage rises by 10 per cent, say, this affects directly 2,000,000 men out of about 47,000,000. Figures for wage and salary earnings are obtainable. Thus marking up the figure for the wage bill in steel, adding this to the previous wage-bill total, and then simply dividing by the number of employees will yield the information on w that we seek.

How the whole economy is then affected depends on what the price of steel does to other prices: how it affects k in the economy. For an industry like steel this can be estimated with fair precision, for the important users of steel are

---

* Department of Commerce data before me indicate that in "Iron and Steel and their products," 1,863,000 were employed in 1947. Later data are not published in this source. For the moment, as only a hypothetical illustration is intended, there is no need for greater precision.

known—e.g., the automobile industry is an obvious one, the construction industry is another, etc.*

There is no need to spell out the details further. Input-output analysis has made all of us cognizant of the interdependence of the economy.† The combination of ideas can permit simpler prediction of the price level impact of sectional and structural wage changes in the future than in the past.

One final remark on this. In practice wage changes in important industries tend to be transmitted soon enough to other sectors of the economy. Suppose they are confined to a few broad industry categories such as Metals and Metal Products (including steel) which employ some 3,500,000, Transportation Equipment employing 1,700,000, Automobiles employing 786,000, Machinery (including electrical) employing 3,000,000, and Railroads employing 1,117,000. This immediately encompasses above 10,000,000 employees, or about one fifth of the total of about 46,600,000. We can see the broad effect, therefore, of a few "key" wage bargains in major industrial groupings in determining the size of w.‡

In ways such as this, the effect of wage agreements on w can be calculated. The "magic constant" k can be given a

---

* It is at this stage that our approach can be grafted on to input-output analysis. Wassily W. Leontief did this in an earlier article where he predicted price changes resulting from wage changes by assuming a constant structure, and thus a constant mark-up. However, he did not, I think, see the implications of his work for price level theory. I think my macroeconomic formulation of the price level ought to permit the tool-users to make important simplifications in securing workable results for practical policy purposes. See, however, his pioneering volume on *The Structure of American Economy* (New York, Oxford, 1951), 2nd ed., pp. 194–196.

† See the fine study of W. Duane Evans and Marvin Hoffenberg, "The Interindustry Relations Study for 1947," *Review of Economics and Statistics* (May 1952).

‡ This confirms several observations I made for aggregation in my *Approach to the Theory of Income Distribution*, especially p. 53.

small flip to account for the extra consequences for the general price level not incorporated directly in w.

The Ultimate Generalization

I shall defer to Chapter 13 the decisive point and key simplification to Price Level Prediction. I call it the "final generalization" of price level theory.

Likewise, I shall withhold a discussion of predicting the income distribution until Chapter 12.

Piecing Together Data

Questions may arise on estimating A; it was observed that this tended to grow at a steady rate and thus did not generally have to be predicted through complex procedures.*

Suppose there is reason to suspect that it has not maintained its historical trend. How can an allowance be made for this? The statistical plenty with which the Commerce Department blesses us comes only at periodic intervals.

Consider the familiar Federal Reserve Board index of Industrial Production; it is well known that this is heavily weighted to reflect manufacturing industry. Movements in this series, compared to our Q for aggregate real output, appear in Table 6.1, from 1947 on.

Clearly these have moved in unison and close juxtaposition: reducing the F.R. series slightly would yield rather full coincidence. Hence the F.R. index could, over the period indicated, serve as a proxy variable for Q. Whenever we have reason to suspect the two are tending to deviate and separate from their pattern for this past period, adjustments could be made through intelligent guess-work.

* Insofar as this is so, another important constant (involving a growth rate) is embraced by the WCM-truism.

TABLE 6.1. FEDERAL RESERVE INDEX OF
INDUSTRIAL PRODUCTION AND THE INDEX
OF AGGREGATE OUTPUT, 1947–1957
(1947–49 = 100)

Year	F.R. Index	Q
1947	100	98
1948	104	102
1949	97	101
1950	112	110
1951	120	117
1952	124	120
1953	134	126
1954	125	124
1955	139	135
1956	143	138
1957	143	139
Average 1947–57	123	119

Information on tendencies of the two indexes to depart can come from a variety of sources: Federal Reserve sector breakdowns, or Commerce or Bureau of Labor Statistics sources. Opportunities for intelligent application of our schematic WCM-truism are legion, defying convenient enumeration.

In the same way, indexes of employment can be concocted. Table 6.2 compares the series of the Bureau of Labor Statistics on nonagricultural employment and our N-series. The confluence, and minor adaptation necessary, are rather patent. In this way, good information seems always capable of being pieced together to give the forecaster a firm line while he casts in an otherwise impenetrable sea. The price level fish can be caught—or one very nearly equivalent in size!

TABLE 6.2. BUREAU OF LABOR STATISTICS INDEX OF
NONAGRICULTURAL EMPLOYMENT AND THE INDEX
OF AGGREGATE EMPLOYMENT, 1947–1957
(1947–49 = 100)

Year	BLS	N
1947.............	99	100
1948.............	102	102
1949.............	99	98
1950.............	102	101
1951.............	108	107
1952.............	110	108
1953.............	114	111
1954.............	111	107
1955.............	114	111
1956.............	118	114
1957.............	119	115
Average 1947–57...	109	107

Which Price Level?

This entire analysis has been devoted so far to the theory
of the general price level, which is the one that economists
talk about, the one which appears in the EOE as well as in
the WCM.

Yet in practice we seem destined to use, on a month-to-
month basis, the index of Consumer Prices and of Wholesale
Commodity Prices, both processed and published in the fine
statistical laboratories of the Bureau of Labor Statistics.

We do not have to use these indexes; we can confine our
predictions to the general price level.* But my guess is that
it will be helpful to associate our index to these commonplace tools for understanding the economy.

First, we may look at all three series before commenting

* That is, of Business Gross Product.

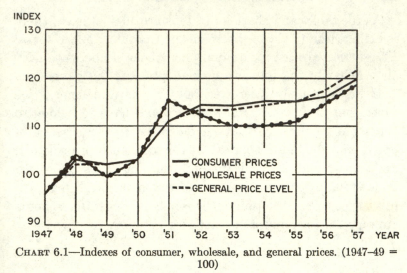

CHART 6.1—Indexes of consumer, wholesale, and general prices. (1947–49 = 100)

on them. They are depicted in Chart 6.1 and the values specified in Table 6.3.

TABLE 6.3. INDEXES OF CONSUMER PRICES, WHOLESALE COMMODITY PRICES, AND THE GENERAL PRICE LEVEL, 1947–1957
(1947–49 = 100)

Year	Consumer Prices	Wholesale Prices	P
1947................	96	96	96
1948................	103	104	102
1949................	102	99	102
1950................	103	103	103
1951................	111	115	111
1952................	114	112	113
1953................	114	110	113
1954................	115	110	114
1955................	115	111	115
1956................	116	114	118
1957................	120	118	122
Average 1947–57......	109	108	109

As the tables and chart indicate, since 1947 at least, there is little reason to choose between the Consumer and General Price series, at least for annual phenomena. Experience with their behavior will indicate how adaptations can be made.

If we were truly interested only in the Consumer Price index, our basic w, A, and k data would have to belong to the same universe as that encompassed by the basket of goods embodied in this index. At the moment it is academic, and superfluous, to indicate how this might be done. An understanding of the argument of this monograph will permit a speedy construction of the requisite conceptual scheme appropriate to the separate indexes.

7

The Wedding Ceremony: Price Level and Aggregate Output

This is the only chapter that is directed primarily to specialists in economics. The rest of the book requires very little formal training. The chapter is brief and these few pages may be omitted without any loss of continuity or essential substance, so far as the theory of the price level goes.

The Wedding Announcement

The announcement that the theory of the price level was to be married to the theory of output in a macroeconomic union was made in the opening pages. The initial arrangements have been made and the brief ceremony can come off. While I have some reservations on whether it is a wholly correct union, I think it may be a fruitful one.

In the previous chapters, some formal equations for the determination of the price level were developed. I think the following two are generally acceptable:

$$P_t = k_t w_t / A_t \tag{7.1}$$

$$k_t = \bar{k} \pm \epsilon \tag{7.2}$$

Economists are likely to be particularly uncomfortable about the equation for A and w. One could argue that historically the A-path has followed a clear course so that there is no reason to fiddle with it. But to show how it can be wrapped into the complete system, and the merger of price level and macroeconomics be fulfilled, the following equations suggest the way out for a tidy solution.

To associate A to the traditional "laws of returns," it is sensible and appropriate to break it down to its determining characteristics. Thus:

$$N_t = N(Q_t, E_{t-1}, I_{t-1}) \tag{7.3}$$

The term E_{t-1} stands for the previous period's stock of capital equipment. I_{t-1} specifies the most recently past burst of investment which will be absorbed into the economy in period t and contribute to productivity improvements. As I_{t-1} embodies the most recent technological improvements, it seems well to siphon it off and keep it distinct from E_{t-1}.

Consider what equation (7.3) does. In effect, it throws equation (7.1) back into the form $P = kwN/Q$, so that we have five variables to deal with. So far there are only three equations.

But we can look further at equation (7.3). As it includes Q, and Q is obviously just a synonymous term for the Y-symbol of real income or output of Keynesian-type theories, it is through Q (or Y) that the link-up with the macroeconomic theory of output can be performed.

Before forging this last link, we would also want to develop the wage equation. However, for various theoretical reasons, I leave this as a largely exogenous specification rather than building in a market equation which reflects the current labor market facts.*

$$w_t = w(w_{t-1}/P_{t-1}, P^*, U_{t-1}) \qquad (7.4)$$

In equation (7.4) the wage is a function of immediate past unemployment, U_{t-1}, the immediate past real wage which affects labor bargaining attitudes, and the expected price level (P^*) which also conditions bargaining decisions. No new variables are introduced in equation (7.4).

For the theory of output I shall use only the simplest and most conventional functions of the neo-Keynesian tradition.†

The income definitional identity is

$$Q_t \equiv Y_t \equiv C_t + I_t \qquad (7.5)$$

C represents, of course, real consumption, while I signifies real investment.

* For the present I have decided on this procedure, for otherwise it would have been necessary to rewrite all of the determining equations in a rather complicated and unfamiliar way in order to arrive at a market-clearing equation for the wage rate. For example, the money wage would have to appear in the equations determining consumption and investment. The whole analysis would have become unduly complex—maybe disproportionate to the practical importance of the matter. I have already argued elsewhere that the effects of changes in the money wage on employment are usually small, in any event. The theoretically more fastidious would thus want to re-work the entire structure of conventional equations. See, e.g., my *Income Distribution*, pp. 128, 129, 167, for an indication of how this might be done. For the present, therefore, I make the money wage a largely exogenous variable, linked functionally to recent past and predicted future events.

† As remarked, I do not agree that these are the sole macroeconomic equations or even the best ones. I think if their full implications were realized by Keynes he would have disavowed them except as an approximate simplification.

The consumption function is written

$$C_t = C(Y_t, r_t) \tag{7.6}$$

where r represents interest rates. Interest-rate phenomena affect not only savings (to a degree) directly, but also consumption purchases via the installment plan indirectly.

$$I_t = I(r_t, R_{t-1}, R^*) \tag{7.7}$$

The R-term stands for profits, recently past and conjectured for the future.

$$L_t = L(r_t, Q_t; P_t) \tag{7.8}$$

This is the demand for money. As written it is novel because the demand for money is made dependent not only on real output but also on the level of prices.* But prices are introduced only as a parametric constant whose value is given by the WCM-truism and the k, w, and A components, where the latter derives from the real system.

The supply of money (M) is an exogenously determined variable, resulting from monetary policy.

$$M_t = \overline{M} \tag{7.9}$$

This is equated, in the market place, to L, the demand for money. Practically, this means simply that there is no direct causal influence of changing money supplies on the price level.†

* Cf. my *Approach to the Theory of Distribution*, pp. 166–167.

† At full employment, conceivably more money would press on interest rates and would lead to more investment and consumption demand without output increasing. But this would mean a *rise* in k. The postwar period shows the opposite phenomenon. Too, all this presupposes easy money policies during full employment!

It is for such unreal cases that EOE arguments have a certain ring of plausibility. Yet their causal nexus and factual foundation are mistaken and inaccurate.

It might also be observed that a "demand-inflation" without a wage rise entails a rising k. But this theory, too, draws scant support from the postwar evidence.

Thus we have 9 equations and 9 unknowns: P_t, k_t, w_t, A_t ($= Q_t/N_t$), C_t, I_t, r_t, L_t ($= M$).

The hook-up thus is complete.

Thoughts About the Ceremony

First, note that a term has been inserted in equation (7.8) to tie the demand for money to the price level. This is long overdue.

The most important aspect of the merger is that money enters into the model only through the interest rate. It has no independent power to affect prices except insofar as it influences the level of output, the level of employment, and, through them, both A and the wage level.

That is to say, the immediate impact of money supplies is on investment and consumption, and thus on Q and N — thus on A, if returns to scale are not constant.*

Through the effect on Q and N, money wages may be influenced. It is through this very indirect path that monetary management influences the price level. It must do its work by pressing on output and employment.

This diagnosis has profound implications for public policy. I comment on these below.

A Technicality in the Union

It is well to reflect further on why the price level must be explicitly honored in the macroeconomic union.

It must be realized that, once the price level is accepted as part of the arrangements, the real phenomena—meaning Q and N—become dependent indirectly on money cost and price level relations. It is a rather ironic fact that Keynesian

---

* I would take the short-period influence on A to be relatively unimportant. In most practical arguments this is assumed to be the case. See the following chapter for further comment.

disciples have omitted this tie in their rush to work with real variables, in C and in I. But this is to revert essentially to the very barter concepts that Keynes deplored; the neo-Keynesians have admitted a (minor?) monetary aspect to enter only through the speculative demand for money.

As the liquidity or money demand function is now written (in Eq. 7.8 above), the price level, and changes in the price level, become a major determinant of the transactions-demand for money. Changes in the level of prices have heretofore been ignored in those systems which make L_t a function of just Q and r: in these formulations the price level, and changes in it, have been neglected, unmentioned poor cousins.

Is there any doubt but that the pressure on money supplies, and thus interest rates, since the 1930's has been due not only to the expansion of output but also to the rise in prices? Output since 1940 has about doubled. The price level has *more* than doubled. Both factors have thus shaped the transactions-demand for cash balances.* Function (7.8) recognizes this.

* Symbolically,

$$\frac{\delta L_t}{\delta P_t} \frac{\delta P_t}{\delta w_t} > 0$$

Thus the interest rate will rise with a rise in the price level, which itself is a function of the money wage level.

8

The Eclipse of the
Equation of Exchange

In the history of science new theories have replaced old not for the sake of change but because they were better: the old theories were inadequate for the explanation of important phenomena, and thus for predictive application.

I think I have provided a better formalization of the price level ingredients and a better theory of price level movements than can be derived from the Equation of Exchange. Why?

The Money Supply Is *Not* a Useful Price Lever

Even for those not tainted with a crude quantity theory, the upshot is that once they begin with the EOE they are bound to argue, sooner or later, that the way to control the price level is to control the money supply.

According to the WCM-equation, the price level cannot fall unless k, w, or A varies. Does M operate on k?

No.

Does it operate on w? But how? Can the Federal Reserve Board sit in on collective bargaining agreements? If not, I conclude it cannot affect w—except through indirect means.

To this the usual retort of EOE theorists is that if banks deny business firms the money they can't pay higher wages.

This is a fallacy. Without ample funds business firms will curb labor hire and reduce their output. They *can* pay a higher wage per man to those who remain employed—if they are pressed by market forces to do it.

Any business, no matter how limited its funds, can always pay some men more by dismissing other employees.

I conclude that this argument that restrictive money supplies directly reduce money wages is based on a fallacy, pure and simple. The modus operandi of monetary policy is different. Its influence is on Q, and through Q, on N, and in this way, on w. The path of influence on prices is indirect, not direct, as has been claimed by EOE theorists.

There is no way of curbing price inflation except through the relation w/A, and through this Ratio alone. Operating on M carries its punch on the roundabout, obliquely rather than directly.

The Strange Denial of a Wage-Price Spiral

EOE theorists also deny frequently that there can be a wage-price spiral. The ordinary man sees this, and my WCM-truism formalizes it. But the EOE proponents profess that it is an illusion.

As I understand it, the wage-price spiral merely means that a rise in wages will generate a rise in prices (unless A goes up). According to our WCM-identity, this seems unexceptional.*

It could be put the other way. If prices rise in t_1, then wage earners will, through their unions, seek a rise in t_2. This will

---

* Cf. the useful study by Prof. A. J. Brown, *The Great Inflation, 1939–1951* (London, Oxford Univ. Press, 1955), Ch. 4. Professor Brown gives more weight to the demand side of a wage rise as a price lever than I think warranted. My stress is on cost movements as the spiraling factor.

push prices up, then wages, etc. The process would continue until some brake was put on the wage rise, directly or indirectly.*

Why the EOE denial? Largely, their argument seems to be that P cannot rise without M or V going up, or Q going down. But this is a curious—and false—argument. For wages *can* go up, and prices *can* go up. Perhaps V also goes up simultaneously. But is it more valid to state that it was V that "caused" the price rise?

This is confusing and mystifying reasoning, accepting an obscure and pedantic formulation rather than a direct and obvious explanation.

Why academic folk—and some Federal Reserve authorities—prefer labored to obvious explanations is a never-ending source of mystery and bewilderment. Only if simple facts can be made complicated do they seem willing to try to understand them.

The EOE Is Not a Predictive Theory

Much the worse shortcoming of the EOE is that it leads to no truly useful predictive theory of the price level.

Consider its evasions. Will an increase in M raise prices? Well, if V and Q don't change.

Will a change in Q affect prices? Only if V and M don't change.

How about a change in V?—the rest of the answer can be filled in.

It is fair to ask whether the WCM is better in these respects. The answer is an affirmative, primarily because of the

* The well-known study of the classic German inflation by C. Bresciani-Turroni is disappointing, on reexamination, because of its neglect of wage movements. See *The Economics of Inflation* (London, Allen and Unwin, 1937), M. Sayers, trans. With her usual perspicacity Mrs. Robinson noted the omission of the wage-price spiral in her brief review (*Economic Journal* [Sept. 1938], p. 150.)

"magic k" and, maybe, the almost similar magic growth rate that seems built in A. Thus we *can* say that a rise in money wages will elevate prices, with only a slight demurrer by way of reservation about the ϵ-tail in k, and a little more skepticism about A. Surely, if we just go back and take another quick look at Table 3.4, we see that, next to Q, A is a veritable constant.

The A-series ranged from a low of 70 to a high of 122. The Q-series ran all the way from 41 to 139. There are some complimentary things, then, that can be said about the sobriety and the steadfastness of the WCM-term A that cannot be candidly said for its EOE counterpart Q.

The Instability of V

How, then, goes V? Is it nearly constant like k?

Nothing need be said about M. It is an exogenous variable, meaning about as easy—less so, I think—to predict as w. For to predict M is to anticipate all the turns and maneuvers in monetary policy, in response to seasonal, temporary, ephemeral, or even durable phenomena. It is much easier, in my opinion, to guess the course of w. But this is an opinion. Economic theory *does* take M as an outside, or exogenous, variable. It does take w as an inside, or endogenous, variable.* On this one, settled theory has resolved any current serious dispute.

Let us look at V. This is usually defined to mean the number of times each piece of money circulates and becomes somebody's money income. It is computed in a way similar to that which we used for k, though this time the value of money output (PQ) is divided by M. Actually, PQ is not

* That is, in a full system, even though, in the previous chapter, I short-cut the analysis in the interests of some brevity. Considering the labor unions' influence on the labor supply curve, I do think that accurate predictions about w are more nearly possible than about M.

the income concept used; the national income concept is preferred because of the definition of V as "income velocity."

As a result of Mr. Selden's work, it has been possible to put the V-series in index form. This appears alongside the k-series, for easy comparability. k, I might add, has also been placed on a national income basis (K_y). There was no

TABLE 8.1. INDEX OF INCOME VELOCITY OF MONEY (V_y)
AND OF THE RATIO OF NATIONAL INCOME TO EMPLOYEE
COMPENSATION (K_y), 1929–1951
(1947–49 = 100)

Year	V_y*	K_y
1929	123	112
1930	106	105
1931	85	97
1932	66	89
1933	67	88
1934	77	93
1935	83	99
1936	88	98
1937	96	100
1938	87	97
1939	88	98
1940	93	102
1941	108	105
1942	126	105
1943	122	101
1944	107	98
1945	86	95
1946	83	99
1947	95	99
1948	105	102
1949	101	99
1950	109	101
1951	122	100

* Computed from Richard T. Selden, "Monetary Velocity in the United States," in *Studies in the Quantity Theory of Money* (University of Chicago Press, 1956), Milton Friedman, editor, p. 200.

need to do this because I want to use the k-factor only for gross product ideas. However, to avoid a show of strictly no contest, it has been done in this way, to put the velocity-mark-up comparison in the most favorable light for the former. (See Table 8.1.)

The rather mercurial nature of V_y to K_y hardly requires comment. The former moved over a range of 66 to 126; the latter, of 88 to 112. The largest year-to-year change in V_y was 21; in K_y it was 8. Chart 8.1 makes the "invidious" comparison.

In a more recent article, Selden has also computed that V_y rose by 13 per cent in the few years between the end of 1954 and 1957.* I conclude that the velocity component of the EOE is not a firm foundation on which to erect a predictive price level theory. The whole structure will topple down if we try.

A Valuable Insight for a Predictive Science

With the insight with which he is gifted, Professor Friedman, in a very recent writing† in the monetary area, has remarked:

One of the chief reproaches directed at economics as an allegedly empirical science is that it can offer so few numerical "constants," that it has isolated so few fundamental regularities.

* "Cost-Push," *op. cit.*, p. 6. Curiously, Selden seems to think the variability of V is a virtue of the EOE for it helps him "explain" inflation: thus, "the recent inflation has resulted from a strong upsurge in velocity" (p. 19). It would be more correct to state that it was "accompanied by," and not carry a misleading causal connotation. To say it was "accompanied by" a rise in velocity is true enough, but not more significant than Calvin Coolidge's purported remark that "you have unemployment when people are out of work." From a tautology only tautologies can be derived.

† All of the quotations come from one paragraph in Milton Friedman, "The Quantity Theory of Money—A Restatement," pp. 20–21, in *Studies in the Quantity Theory of Money*. It need hardly be said that I regard Professor Friedman's restatement of this theory to be the best of those with which I am familiar.

This statement is unexceptional—and eloquent: it coincides with several of my remarks earlier in this work. Ironically, Professor Friedman then declares:

The field of money is the chief example one can offer in rebuttal: there is perhaps no other empirical relation in economics that has been observed to recur so uniformly under so wide a variety of circumstances as the relation ... in the stock of money and in prices; the one is invariably linked with the other and is in the same direction; this uniformity is, I suspect, of the same order as many of the uniformities that form the basis of the physical sciences.

His observations then lead him to say:

And the uniformity is in more than direction. There is an extraordinary empirical stability and regularity to such magnitudes as income velocity that cannot but impress anyone who works extensively with monetary data.

Speaking of the articles in the collection of essays which he edited, he feels that "they make, I believe, an important contribution toward extracting this stability and regularity, toward isolating the numerical 'constants' of monetary behavior." The paragraph concludes with the plea that:

It is by this criterion at any rate that I, and I believe also their authors, would wish them to be judged.

There is only one observation that need be made: if there is "an extraordinary empirical stability" to income velocity, if this is a "constant" then k must be regarded as "rigid"! Truly k is the "magical constant." A "bit of a miracle," Keynes once called it.* Chart 8.2 presents a fascinating profile comparison.

* J. M. Keynes, "Relative Movements of Real Wages and Output," *Economic Journal* (1939), pp. 48–49.

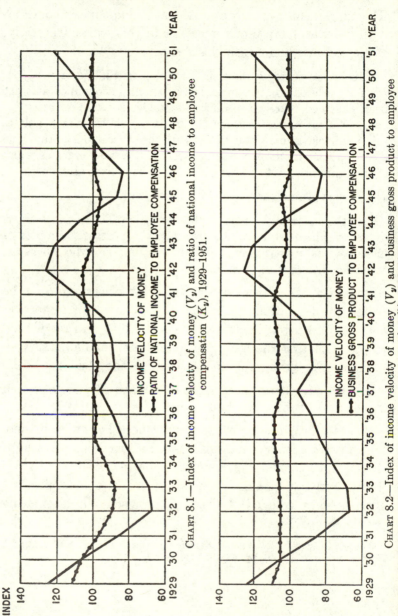

CHART 8.1—Index of income velocity of money (V_y) and ratio of national income to employee compensation (K_y), 1929–1951.

CHART 8.2—Index of income velocity of money (V_y) and business gross product to employee compensation (k) 1929–1951

Conclusions

Some wrong inferences have come from EOE proponents; this is not too bad, for they can be corrected. The failure of the EOE, instead, stems from (1) its believing that an indirect influence (of the money supply) on the price level is a direct one, and hence serving to misguide policy, and (2) its lack of a predictive mechanism. All its explanations are ad hoc and ex post. Ex ante it provides no firm guide lines to events, for its Q oscillates badly compared to A and V, even worse compared to k.

9

A Miscast Federal Reserve

If these arguments are correct (and a professional economist who challenges conventional doctrines must proceed on
this premise), they carry portentous implications for the role
of the Federal Reserve Board of Governors—not the Federal
Reserve Banks whose functions are largely of the service and
routine variety.

Consider the situation. The Federal Reserve Board is the
main, if not the only, discretionary agency with delegated
power to stabilize the economy. To accomplish this worthy
end it has been handed control over the money supply.

The irony of this is that the Federal Reserve accepts the
responsibility without realizing how badly it has been mis-
cast for a role to which its talents are unsuited. Invariably
its officials spend lengthy and arduous afternoons before
Congressional Committees explaining how well it has done
and how wise it has been and is being. Yet the Congressmen
always ask the same question; namely, why the economy is
unstable, teetering on inflation or tottering on recession. In
the last two years it has done both, teetered and tottered,
with recession in employment, output, income, and profits,
and inflation in prices.

Is there any wonder at these results? I think not. As
directly as I can state it, the Federal Reserve is not equipped
to combat inflation. Its operations take place via the money

supply whereby it can exercise influence on the volume of lending, and thus, investment and consumption.

But it does not—and we would not want it to—sit in on the wage negotiations. Thus it has no way of preventing prices from rising when wages rise—unless it tightens money, accomplishes unemployment, and eases the labor market.

It can thus—temporarily—avoid inflation, but at the awesome cost of unemployment. It is not entirely coincidental that the three postwar recessions were accompanied by "tight money." I refer to 1949, 1953, and 1957–58.

This is not to allege that the Reserve officials are willful men or that they deliberately bring on recession, or "cause" it. The officials are devoted public servants manfully trying to fulfill their responsibilities. They draw on copious statistics to learn where the economy is going. Yet we still have imbalance. The fault is not with the men: it is rather with their tools. The real criticism is that they have not realized they have been short-changed: a hard confession for any banker to make!

The point: a brake on monetary policy is a brake on output primarily, and only indirectly an impediment on prices.

It can safely be predicted that, over the future, the Chairman of the Federal Reserve, whoever he may be, will be continually fighting inflation—or deflation. He cannot expect much respite except by fortuitous, favorable accidents, such as a sharp rise in A because of spectacular improvements in technology.

The Impossibility of a Quiet Life

The reason why a quiet life is not possible for the Federal Reserve ought to be apparent. Whenever the System "fights" inflation, it leads to deflation. As it combats deflation through easy money, as in late 1954 and early 1958, it must prepare its stance against inflation. It is like a poor boxer mismatched against two opponents simultaneously in the prize ring. He is bounced from one to the other without let-up.

Rather than recognizing the futility of its tight-rope act, one in which it is constantly falling off the wire, the Reserve System has come to rationalize its misfortunes by arguing that it is somehow succeeding in stabilizing the system— even when we have no stability. Vices, when viewed as virtues, make life tolerable, so it seems. Most of us can recognize this.

Does Control Over Inflation Control Inflation?

A serious question may be raised as to whether the Federal Reserve's fight over inflation does really combat inflation. Or is this a delusion too?

Monetary policy, I claim, has its incidence on output and employment. As a result, pressure on wages is relieved and, through this channel, the price level is held in check.

But how about the consequences for the longer pull? The restraint on output means a slowing up of the pace of investment. As investment is retarded, the growth of productivity in the economy is slowed down, to a canter if not a halt. This does mean that the A-factor in the WCM-equation is slowed down, held from rising so quickly.

But a slowing down in capital formation, a repression in A, must operate to lift prices over time compared to their levels if A was permitted to grow naturally in an economy of full employment and stability.

Thus the price of present inflation control is a loss of a future inflation deterrent. It is doubtful, on this appraisal, if the Fed's price level accomplishments have been worth the noise, the acrimony, or the drag on the economy that has been exercised.

The Federal Reserve officials have tended to characterize their actions as "leaning against the wind" in order to achieve stability. On the basis of this diagnosis, the immediate wind-break builds up a future storm for present price level deflation is paid for with some future price level inflation. "You pays your money and takes your choice."

The Function of the Federal Reserve

Our criticism of the Federal Reserve has been of the incompatibility between the job and the tools allotted. Man may get to the Moon in a rocket, not a rocking chair. The wage level, not the money supply, governs the price level.

This lays open the question of the proper role for the Federal Reserve. Largely, in an economy which does not use the older metallic standards, such as gold, it is necessary to have an agency to provide for increases in the supply of money over time in order to maintain maximum employment and resource use at the agreed-upon price level. On this interpretation there is a permanent job for the Federal Reserve, maybe not as big a one as it has conceived itself of having in the past, still, not a small one.*

But the Federal Reserve, with the power to cut off or augment money supplies, is a poor instrument for achieving economic stability.†

* Its other job is to eliminate expectations of inflation by refusing to ease money supplies when employment is full. In this sense it conditions the expectational parameter P^* in equation (7.4).

† Because I have expressed myself at more length on this subject elsewhere, I may be permitted the levity of condensing this discussion. See my article, "Monetary Policy or Wage Policy: The Dilemma of the Federal Reserve," *The Bankers' Magazine* (London), 1958. Cf. E. S. Shaw, "Monetary Stability in a Growing Economy," in *Allocation of Economic Resources*, Essays in Honor of B. F. Haley (Stanford Univ. Press, 1959). I largely accept Shaw's position on money and growth though I would give more weight to "liquidity preference proper" than he does in this article.

10

Wage Policy: A Way Out

If monetary policy and a great central bank cannot control inflation without leading us to recession, what is the way out?

Control over M has been pooh-poohed. The other important variables may be enumerated, and eliminated in order.

V—there is no way of controlling this, as Selden tells us. It takes us up or down over time. It never holds us very stable.

A, average productivity, is likewise beyond direct influence, as are N and Q. About all a government can do with either, aside from creating a favorable tax climate and price level—employment stability, is to exhort. But this influence blows quick and wears short.

The "magic constant" k seems safely beyond our reach. This leaves only w as a possibility.*

Watch-Tower Control

Does this mean that government must sit in on all collective bargaining negotiations, or approve all wage increases,

* That great central banker, Allan Sproul, formerly President of the Federal Reserve Bank of New York, sensed this as well as the futility of trying to prevent price increases after wage increases through the agency of monetary control. See his remarks at the University of California, Berkeley, May 10, 1958.

or hamstring the economy with new red tape and another agency for filing questionnaires?

At the present time I think that all that would be called for would be a research agency collecting data on all (important) wage agreements, and estimating what their implications are for the price level by means of the tools staked out above. Once this information was available, and once union leaders knew that it was possible for Congress to call for it and legislate in the hue and cry over inflation, I think the situation would do much to correct itself. The topside in the labor movement would know that a check was being kept on its demands, that the price level consequences were being adjudged. This alone would counsel restraint.

Businessmen, too, would come to appreciate that they might have to explain excessive wage bargains which were paid for by market price increases.

I think, too, that this information not only ought to be gathered by a central agency organized specifically for the task—and it could be a *small* agency for the number of important and significant wage agreements are few—but also it should be published, available to all students of our economy, to permit them to draw the correct inferences on why prices rose.

All that I am suggesting is that in this sphere we need something akin to the watchful eye of either the Anti-Trust Division in the Attorney General's office or else the Federal Trade Commission. A watchtower approach alone is intended. No powers other than a research chore ought to be delegated to the agency. Responsibility for policy would remain with the Congress. The power it possesses to make laws, and the knowledge that good information is at hand to provide the groundwork for legislation, would do much to rectify the absurdity of events of recent years where wages and prices, and prices and wages, have been chasing one another in a widening circle.

What is suggested is moderate, very much so. Many will contend in advance that it will prove ineffective. Maybe so. The proof must come *after* the doing. The undertaking will not be expensive while any success it may achieve can only redound to the general benefit. Not only might there be a prevention of the continuance of the inflationary tendencies, but it would also create an environment in which monetary policy can succeed in doing the only job for which it is cut out to do directly, namely, to influence Q and N.

The Liberal Muddle

So-called liberal thinkers have been in a muddle over this issue. They have sensed that the Federal Reserve was not succeeding; also they have not been unaware of wage pressures. And yet, rather than face the question head on, they have ducked it. Many, instead, have veered around full circle to declare themselves openly in favor of "mild" inflation.

Of course, much depends on definitions, of whether price level increases of 1 per cent or so per annum are talked about or, as between 1950 and 1957, some 19 per cent over this period is in mind. This is a rate of 2.7 per cent per year. I think this excessive for it serves little purpose while it does cause some distress.

Hence, anyone criticizing the Federal Reserve for its (misguided) stabilization and anti-inflation maneuvers must accept, sooner or later, the need for restraining the growth in wage rates. Otherwise inflation as a way of life is being offered merely to avoid disturbing the bargaining exactions of union leaders and businessmen either unconcerned about or uninformed on the price level consequences of their acts.

Appeal to Reason

We need an agency for collecting the facts and organizing them, as I have suggested. This may be enough to do the job against inflation. Then the Federal Reserve could exercise its proper influence against deflation.

If this doesn't work we will have the basis for slightly sterner measures. At the present time there is no way of deciding readily on the magnitude of the problem or of having the bargaining agents appreciate the price level consequences contingent upon their actions.

The real reason why so moderate a policy has every chance of succeeding in the future, while it would have failed in the past, is because we now have developed what I think to be the correct theory. In the past, union leaders could plunge ahead with money wage demands, and see them acceded to by business, because both could decide that inflation was someone else's child. That is, practical men, pondering like academic people on the EOE, might have held the Federal Reserve responsible. Or the unions, and apologists, could blame "monopolies." Our analysis showing k rather rigid—even lower in the 1950's than in the 1930's—throws this chestnut back into the fire, for final burning.

A correct theory may work some partial miracles. It can lead to restraint and to reason. Union leaders can never again evade price level responsibility for any immoderate wage change exactions.

11

Decomposing k

Earlier, the desirability of refining k, to look at its major components, was mentioned. Let us do this now.

We shall look at the following series:

1. Rental Income of Persons
2. Net Interest
3. Income of Unincorporated Enterprises and Inventory Valuation Adjustment
4. Corporate Profits and Inventory Valuation Adjustment
5. Corporate Profits Before Tax
6. Corporate Profits Tax Liability
7. Corporate Profits After Tax
8. Indirect Business Tax and Nontax Liability
9. Capital Consumption Allowances

All of the original data on which the calculations were made came from p. 134 of the *U.S. Income and Output* (1959), published by the Department of Commerce. The Compensation of Employees data all refer to Compensation from Business Gross Product.

We shall find some interesting results leading readily to predictive work on income distribution.

At the close of the chapter I want to talk of a "crazy" chart I have had drawn and its significance for economics.

Rental Income of Persons

Table 11.1 compares the Rental Income of Persons to the figures on the Compensation of Employees.

The results in Table 11.1, since 1933 at least, speak for themselves.

TABLE 11.1. THE RENTAL INCOME OF PERSONS
TO EMPLOYEE COMPENSATION, 1929–1957

Year	Ratio
1929	0.12
1930	0.12
1931	0.11
1932	0.10
1933	0.08
1934	0.06
1935	0.06
1936	0.05
1937	0.05
1938	0.07
1939	0.07
1940	0.07
1941	0.07
1942	0.07
1943	0.06
1944	0.06
1945	0.07
1946	0.07
1947	0.06
1948	0.06
1949	0.07
1950	0.07
1951	0.06
1952	0.06
1953	0.06
1954	0.06
1955	0.06
1956	0.05
1957	0.06

Net Interest

Next, consider the data on Net Interest paid out by business enterprises.*

TABLE 11.2. THE NET INTEREST ORIGINATING IN
BUSINESS TO EMPLOYEE COMPENSATION,
1929–1957

Year	Ratio
1929	0.10
1930	0.11
1931	0.14
1932	0.18
1933	0.18
1934	0.15
1935	0.13
1936	0.12
1937	0.10
1938	0.11
1939	0.10
1940	0.08
1941	0.06
1942	0.05
1943	0.04
1944	0.03
1945	0.03
1946	0.02
1947	0.03
1948	0.02
1949	0.03
1950	0.03
1951	0.03
1952	0.03
1953	0.03
1954	0.03
1955	0.03
1956	0.03
1957	0.03

Can a series possibly hold more firmly than this, since 1944?

* This is from the "Income Originating in Business" series.

TABLE 11.3. PROPRIETOR INCOME IN UNINCORPORATED
ENTERPRISES TO EMPLOYEE COMPENSATION,
1929–1957

Year	Ratio
1929	0.34
1930	0.29
1931	0.27
1932	0.21
1933	0.24
1934	0.26
1935	0.35
1936	0.31
1937	0.33
1938	0.32
1939	0.30
1940	0.31
1941	0.33
1942	0.35
1943	0.35
1944	0.34
1945	0.37
1946	0.39
1947	0.33
1948	0.34
1949	0.30
1950	0.29
1951	0.29
1952	0.27
1953	0.26
1954	0.24
1955	0.23
1956	0.21
1957	0.21

Proprietors' Income of Unincorporated Enterprises and Inventory Valuation Adjustment

Table 11.3 conveys the same information for the Income of Unincorporated Enterprises.

In this, as students of this category are aware, there is more instability. And yet it is small enough to serve many predictive purposes.

Corporate Profits Before Tax and Inventory Valuation Adjustment

We now consider the important series on Corporate Profits Before Tax and Inventory Valuation Adjustment. The total of this has amounted to some $40 billions in recent years.

The growth in these figures since the 1930's is rather apparent. The changing tax load is an undoubted contributing factor. There has been good stability in recent years.

Corporate Profits Before Tax, Tax Liability, and After Tax

Let us look more closely at the Corporate Profits category. In Table 11.5 this is broken down into the Profits Before Tax (column 1), the Tax Liability (column 2), and After Tax (column 3).

There is flux here too; the large difference since the 1930's is reflected in the aggregate figures and in Column 2, the Tax Liability computations. After tax, the improvement since 1932, and the move back closer to the 1929 level, is apparent.

Indirect Business Tax and Nontax Liability

The figures representing the Indirect Business Tax liabilities of business firms, which include all the sales and excise taxes, are gathered in Table 11.6. They tell a strong story of stability, one not wholly expected.

TABLE 11.4. CORPORATE PROFITS AND INVENTORY
VALUATION ADJUSTMENT TO EMPLOYEE
COMPENSATION, 1929–1957

Year	Ratio
1929	0.22
1930	0.16
1931	0.05
1932	0.07*
1933	0.09*
1934	0.03
1935	0.09
1936	0.15
1937	0.16
1938	0.11
1939	0.14
1940	0.21
1941	0.27
1942	0.29
1943	0.29
1944	0.27
1945	0.22
1946	0.18
1947	0.21
1948	0.25
1949	0.24
1950	0.27
1951	0.27
1952	0.23
1953	0.21
1954	0.19
1955	0.22
1956	0.21
1957	0.19

* Denotes Losses instead of Profits.

TABLE 11.5. CORPORATE PROFITS BEFORE TAX,
THE TAX LIABILITY, AND AFTER TAX TO
EMPLOYEE COMPENSATION, 1929–1957

Year	(1)	(2)	(3)
1929	0.21	0.03	0.18
1930	0.08	0.02	0.06
1931	0.02*	0.02	0.04*
1932	0.12*	0.02	0.13*
1933	0.01	0.02	0.01*
1934	0.06	0.03	0.03
1935	0.10	0.03	0.06
1936	0.17	0.06	0.11
1937	0.16	0.04	0.12
1938	0.09	0.03	0.06
1939	0.16	0.04	0.12
1940	0.21	0.06	0.15
1941	0.32	0.14	0.17
1942	0.31	0.17	0.14
1943	0.30	0.17	0.13
1944	0.27	0.15	0.12
1945	0.22	0.12	0.10
1946	0.24	0.10	0.14
1947	0.27	0.11	0.16
1948	0.27	0.11	0.17
1949	0.22	0.09	0.13
1950	0.31	0.14	0.17
1951	0.28	0.15	0.13
1952	0.23	0.12	0.10
1953	0.22	0.13	0.10
1954	0.19	0.10	0.09
1955	0.24	0.12	0.12
1956	0.22	0.11	0.11
1957	0.20	0.10	0.10

Note: Column (1) represents Before Tax.
Column (2) represents Tax Liability.
Column (3) represents After Tax.

* Denotes Losses.

TABLE 11.6. INDIRECT TAXES AND NONTAX LIA-
BILITIES TO EMPLOYEE COMPENSATION, 1929–1957

Year	Ratio
1929	0.16
1930	0.18
1931	0.21
1932	0.27
1933	0.30
1934	0.29
1935	0.28
1936	0.26
1937	0.23
1938	0.23
1939	0.24
1940	0.24
1941	0.21
1942	0.18
1943	0.16
1944	0.17
1945	0.19
1946	0.19
1947	0.17
1948	0.17
1949	0.19
1950	0.19
1951	0.18
1952	0.18
1953	0.18
1954	0.18
1955	0.18
1956	0.18
1957	0.18

This figure seems to have got stuck at 0.18!

Capital Consumption Allowances

We come now to the important item of Capital Consumption Allowances which, for the most part, comprise depreciation charges.

TABLE 11.7. CAPITAL CONSUMPTION ALLOWANCES
TO EMPLOYEE COMPENSATION, 1929–1957

Year	Ratio
1929	0.20
1930	0.22
1931	0.25
1932	0.39
1933	0.31
1934	0.26
1935	0.25
1936	0.22
1937	0.20
1938	0.22
1939	0.21
1940	0.19
1941	0.17
1942	0.15
1943	0.13
1944	0.14
1945	0.15
1946	0.12
1947	0.12
1948	0.13
1949	0.15
1950	0.07
1951	0.15
1952	0.15
1953	0.16
1954	0.17
1955	0.18
1956	0.19
1957	0.18

For recent years a guess of 0.17 plus or minus 1 or 2 points would have fit rather neatly.

The Constancy of the Components

Examining these data which involve mark-ups for the various nonwage incomes derived from Business Gross Product, we again seem close to some inscrutable law, some unsuspected order. They point the way to an empirically oriented macroeconomic theory of distribution and again suggest that theorists have been remiss in failing to provide explanations for this stability.* We shall say more of this in the next chapter.

The Criss-Cross Charts

Before opening up the macroeconomic theory of distribution to which this points, let us consider Charts 11.1 and 11.2.

Our examination has shown that there is manifest stability in the macroeconomic data. When we come down to the individual industry level it is known that this inner stability does not evidence itself; there is endless movement and fluctuation, and boundless diversity. Withal, the universe is marked by constancy and uniformity.

Bearing on this, we might look at Charts 11.1 and 11.2, originally drawn by me for another study.† When I suggested that these charts be drawn, I was advised not to do so—that they were illegitimate children diagrammatically, that they would be illegible, and that no one could decipher anything from them. But the more one looks at them with the

---

* Some of it is due merely to "small numbers being compared to large." But this is not wholly convincing.

† See my report, *An Examination of Some Economic Aspects of Forest Service Stumpage Prices and Appraisal Policies* (Washington, D. C., U.S. Forest Service, 1958).

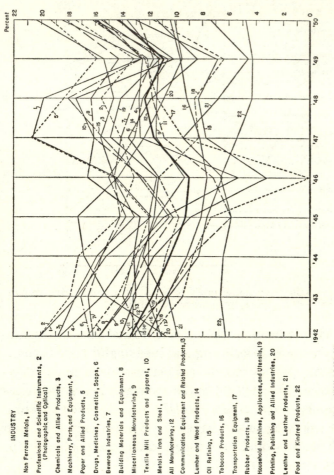

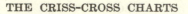

CHART 11.1—Operating profit as a percentage of sales for listed manufacuring corporations, 1942–1950.

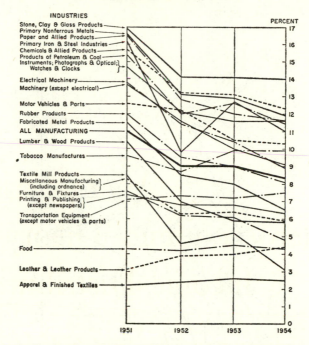

CHART 11.2—Ratio of operating profit to sales, all manufacturing corporations, by industry, 1951–1954.

macroeconomic facts on the price level and income division in mind, the more fascinating and meaningful they become. The lines go up, they run down in criss-cross fashion, crazy-quilt pattern. Through it all the movements stay within a limited range. There is order in this crazy complex; there is some law applying to the units—if we could only reach out and grab it we would have more ideas comparable to the physical sciences.

12

An Empirical Macroeconomic Theory of Income Distribution

The results of the last chapter permit us to take large steps toward an empirically oriented macroeconomic theory of income distribution. The relations indicate the way in which the income pattern works out, rather than providing an explanation of it. This is the task of theory.

Rental Income

Writing Y_1 for the Rental Income of Persons from Business Proceeds, and wN for the Compensation of Employees out of the same proceeds, then:

$$Y_1 = (0.06 + \theta_1)wN \qquad \textbf{(12.1)}$$

The term θ_1 denotes a possible (minor) variation from 0.06 for Y_1. In recent years (since about 1934) it has been practically zero—or 0.01 up or down.

Proprietor's Income

Noting Proprietor's Income of Unincorporated Enterprises (and Inventory Valuation Adjustment) by Y_2, then:

$$Y_2 = (0.25 + \theta_2)wN \qquad (12.2)$$

Since about 1949, θ_2 has been ± 0.05 or less.

Corporate Profits

For Corporate Profits Before Tax,

$$Y_3 = (0.25 + \theta_3)wN \qquad (12.3)$$

For this case, too, since 1943 a range of θ of ± 0.05 would cover the facts.

Just stating the numerical values of the parenthetical term, the Corporate Tax Liability could be estimated in the same way, as about (0.12 ± 0.03). For Corporate Profits After Tax, a value of (0.12 ± 0.05) would have covered all the cases since 1939.

The business income proceeds allotted to indirect taxes and miscellaneous nontax liabilities seems to have become stuck at about a value of (0.18 ± 0.02) since 1942. Since 1951 the figure 0.18 would have done the trick. Net Interest business payments have recently settled firmly at 0.03.

Capital Consumption Allowances

Since 1951 the Capital Consumption Allowances compared to the Employee Compensation totals have hovered within (0.17 ± 0.03).

The Wage Share

The wage share, according to the evidence, has tended to be almost exactly half of the Business Gross Proceeds.

Useful Predictive Tools

I think these results are useful as predictive tools. The steadiness over several years of the recent past suggests they are not likely to be quickly upset. From various bits of side data it ought to be possible to do a bit more to make intelligent estimates of the directional move in θ and to narrow the range of variation. Those more adept at curve fitting, I think, could secure forecasts of high accuracy for practically any predictive purposes. Although this has not been demonstrated, much of it, we can surmise intuitively, is due to the "magic k."

13

A Final Price Level Generalization

We can now state what might be described as "the final price level generalization."

Writing $P = kw/A$, the portion w/A represents the money wage divided by the number of units of output per employee. It is thus the wage cost per unit of output.

Once we put $k = 2$ in the equation $P = kw/A$, we have

$$P = 2w/A \qquad \text{(13.1)}$$

Simply translated, this means that prices, or the price level for our purposes, will rise by .02 cents for each .01 cent increase in wage costs per unit of output, or by \$2 for each \$1 increase in unit wage costs. This refers, of course, to a typical "dollar amount" of product turned out in the Business Sector of the economy.

This is a shorthand simplification of vast importance, of direct application in prediction and policy. As we know, k has ranged about 1.90 ± 0.04 since 1952. So long as it stays in this range—and, considering its descent since 1950 this seems probable, unless unusual phenomena are afoot in the economy—it becomes a very easy matter to predict with very high exactitude the consequences for the price level of changes in unit wage costs.

One further major implication of this: If, through improved technology, unit wage costs are reduced .01 cent, then with k rather constant, prices will tend to drop by close to .02 cents.

This is a result never reached or even suggested by the EOE. It indicates the wide range and deep penetrative power of the WCM-formulation.

14

The Price Level Over Time: The Final Synthesis for a Growing Economy

We are now ready for the final step, the synthesis and union of the theory of growth and the theory of the price level. With this it becomes possible to fix the course of the price level in a growing economy.

I shall adopt the growth formula advanced by R. F. Harrod:*

$$G = \frac{s}{C} \tag{14.1}$$

In equation (14.1), G denotes the relative growth of output, or $\Delta Q/Q$.

The term s refers to the average rate of savings. In our formulation this refers to the savings out of business proceeds by all the income recipients sharing in this common

* R. F. Harrod, *Towards a Dynamic Economics* (London, Macmillan and Co., Ltd., 1948), p. 77. See the alternative formulation in E. Domar, *Essays in the Theory of Economic Growth* (New York, Oxford Univ. Press, 1957), Essays III, IV, V.

pool. Thus, $s = S/Z$, where S is the absolute savings sum and Z represents proceeds.

The C-term indicates the dollar amount of equipment used per unit of output. It means, therefore, $I/\Delta Q$, where I stands for investment and ΔQ for the change in real output (per annum, when annual data are used).

Now,

$$Q = A \cdot N \tag{14.2}$$

We are now ready to substitute for $1/A$ in the growth truism equation (14.1), inasmuch as

$$G = \Delta Q/Q = \Delta Q/AN \cdot \tag{14.3}$$

Hence,

$$\frac{\Delta Q}{A \cdot N} = \frac{s}{C} \tag{14.4}$$

and

$$\frac{1}{A} = \frac{s}{C\Delta Q/N} \tag{14.5}$$

We can now return to our basic price level truism:

$$P = kw/A \tag{14.6}$$

Substituting for $1/A$:

$$P = kw \frac{s}{C\Delta Q/N} \tag{14.7}$$

But $\Delta Q/N$ is the *increase* of output per annum divided by the work force. It is the real output increase per man. Let us call this term b. It means henceforth the per employee output growth rate. Thus:

$$P = \frac{kws}{bC} \qquad (14.8)$$

This is the truism for the price level course in a growing economy, where increases in the stock of equipment and per capita output are taking place. It is the final synthesis between the price level and the phenomena that are responsible for economic growth.

The Predictive Application

The obvious next question is to indicate how the important synthesis of equation (14.8) can be applied. I shall use only some sample values; others can refine them to fit the facts more closely.

The value of k we shall take to be 2. Let us suppose that the average savings out of business proceeds (s) are 20 per cent, or $\frac{1}{5}$. Too, suppose that the amount of equipment needed to produce one unit of output—or $1 worth—is $5. Thus $C = \$5$. It would signify that $500 of equipment is used to provide $100 of sales receipts per annum. Also, suppose that b, the output growth per head, is $200. That is, annual output increases by $10,000,000,000 with a workforce of 50,000,000 employees.

To summarize our approximate (and rough) values:

$$k = 2 \qquad (14.9)$$

$$s = \tfrac{1}{5} \qquad (14.10)$$

$$C = \$5 \qquad (14.11)$$

$$b = \$200 \qquad (14.12)$$

Let us now place these results in our WCM-truism, in the form of equation (14.8):

$$P = \frac{2(\frac{1}{5})w}{(\$200)(\$5)} \qquad (14.13)$$

$$= \frac{2w}{5(\$200)(\$5)}$$

$$= \frac{w}{\$2500} \qquad (14.14)$$

This last result is the one we seek. It means literally that, in an economy of growth, the average price of the average unit of output will be equal to the money wage divided by $2500.

Hence, so long as the denominator is a constant money sum, the price level in a growing economy will also respond to the movement in money wages: as equation (14.14) proves conclusively, even if we have all the other variables of growth, such as b, s, and C, the price level is indeterminate without the money wage. In a growing economy as well as a static economy, the money wage is perched on top of the price level roost.

If we take the growth rate (s/C) as constant over time, the price level will fall as b rises: this would ensue from the more rapid increase in per capita output. A rising growth rate would raise prices unless b also moved proportionately.

The Direct Growth–Price Level Tie-up

To make the growth–price level tie-up even more transparent, equation (14.8) can be thrown into the following form by substituting G for s/C. Thus:

$$P = kwG/b \qquad (14.15)$$

In the equational form (14.15) the hook-up of price level and growth is completed. Hence to overlook the price level in the past historical growth course is in a way equivalent to the use of a crude Quantity Theory of Money, in the sense that it presumes the real growth variables operated independently of wage, mark-up, and per employee output increase (b) phenomena.

Investment and the Price Level

Some further light on the growth process appears if the basic equation is linked to the volume of investment. Thus:

$$P = kw/A = \frac{kwI}{\dfrac{Q\,I}{N}} = kwI_q/I_n \qquad (14.16)$$

In this form both the numerator and the denominator have been multiplied by the investment volume (I) so that I_q denotes investment per unit of output, and I_n, investment per unit of employment.

The final form of Eq. 14.16 conveys some new information. It permits us to infer: (1) So long as equipment per head grows faster than equipment per unit of output, then the price level will fall. In the situation implicit in this theorem capital per unit of employment is advancing to offset ordinary diminishing returns phenomena. Hence the price level will be lower, if k and w are unchanged, while living standards face a prospective rise. This case is also compatible with more leisure and a reduced work-week, and hence a retarded pace of output growth in Q. Investment, in a sense, replaces labor in the underlying productive pattern.

In the alternate case (2) where $I_q > I_n$, the price level will rise when k and w hold firm. In this instance presumably population and labor force (N) is growing faster than output (Q), so that the investment relations emerge as stated. Equipment per head would thus be tending to fall and the output increase would be due primarily to more hands—that is, labor—rather than to more equipment. The price level consequence would be exactly what we would expect in this concatenation of essentially classical diminishing returns associated with a relatively excessive rate of growth in the labor force, and only partially alleviated by the equipment growth.

Growth and Income Division

The same set of ideas can be extended to probe more deeply into the relations between income distribution and growth. From Eq. 14.15 we can write:

$$G = Pb/wk \qquad (14.17)$$

It is convenient to break $b = \Delta Q/N$ into its two components, of added consumption output (ΔC) and the increment of investment output (ΔI) so that $\Delta Q = \Delta C + \Delta I$, and $b = (\Delta C/N) + (\Delta I/N)$, or $b = b_c + b_i$.

The importance of this split-up and isolation of b-components becomes more apparent when it is realized that for further growth the added investment sum ΔI signifies new equipment and new capital instruments for further mechanization of the productive process, whereas ΔC entails immediate consumption goods and currently heightened real income in consumption. In general, if we regard the tendency to save out of wage incomes to be nil (or very small), growth in an economy in which real wages and the wage share is high will tend to be realized almost wholly in more consumption goods output. Hence further growth over time will be slower than where savings propensities are higher or in general, where the income shift is more solidly directed against wage-earning groups. A low wage share and high savings are thus capable of raising *future* real wages; low savings and high real wages currently can stymie future improvements in the real wage: present high standards are the recompense for somewhat lower future living standards than might otherwise be attainable.

To illustrate, we can take the two extreme cases, one in which all of the augmented output ΔQ is in the form of consumption goods and one in which the production increment consists entirely of instruments. For the former the growth equation would read:

$$G = Pb_c/wk \qquad (14.18)$$

In this economy we can surmise that the real wage (w/P_c) relation to the b_c term is high so that the growth rate will be small for future time periods inasmuch as with unchanged savings habits only a constant *absolute* amount of the economy's productive resources will be devoted to further investment.*

Conversely, all added output may take the form of extra investment goods. Hence in this case the current real wage remains at its previous level but the prospect brightens for higher future living standards. The relationship is thus of the form:

$$G = Pb_i/wk \qquad (14.19)$$

In this relation if the real wage relation to the b_i term is low, then the growth rate will be larger for the future because of the imminent build-up of instrumental capital goods. Ultimately this sort of economy contains the best

---

* Interestingly, a *fall* in the wage share $(1/k)$ would *lower* G: this is plausible with diminishing returns under pure competition. But b_c would then also be lower, with only the fall in the real wage working to lift G. In this analysis we tread on some intricate interdependencies.

prospect for higher future living standards. Greater absolute amounts of the community's productive resources can go for new investment in this situation.

I think that there are some profound implications which are significant for economic development in these relations. The analyses seem particularly relevant for the growth of the Asian economies and in the battle for economic supremacy of the Western world with the Soviet bloc. Of two economies having the same current annual growth rate, that economy which devotes more of its augmented output to new productive instruments or new productive power will ultimately triumph in the race for higher living standards.* Consuming less of the current output augmentation permits future standards to become progressively higher.

Conclusion

The price level course in a growing economy has now been elucidated. The formalization of the problem has indicated that the growth variables determine the price level only after the money wage is specified.

The equational form (14.8) can thus be fitted to forecasting purposes by adapting more accurate data to replace the hypothetical numbers we have employed in equation (14.13). To predict the price level in index number form, all the necessary series would have to be cast in index number terms.

This is the appropriate procedure for price level forecasts extending into the longer future. It also indicates that any policy which retards the growth of capital, and thus output, will tend to elevate the price level over time.

---

* I think these remarks help illuminate many of the propositions that are puzzling at first brush in Mrs. Joan Robinson's important volume on *The Accumulation of Capital* (Homewood, Ill., Richard Irwin and Co., 1956), Book II, especially p. 90.

Concluding Note

There is no need to recapitulate results at this stage. All of the conclusions can be extracted from the pages above. The thoughts now go to the battleground of ideas, to be challenged, debated, tested by others. I think they will withstand the stern inner criticism they are about to receive. Whatever the outcome, the effort will not be in vain if the result is to make our science as respectable as the physical sciences in which such enormous advances were being made while we were marking time in attacking some important problems of our economy.

Before too much time elapses I hope to make available studies to demonstrate that the price level has behaved over the longer past in the way our basic growth formula suggests. Considering that the formulation descends from the basic truism, I think we are entitled to be confident of the results.

Index